THE

LOCK OF HAIR
[1872]
BY ALEXANNA SPEIGHT

LACIS
PUBLICATIONS
BERKELEY, CA 94703 USA

THE LOCK OF HAIR:

ITS HISTORY, ANCIENT AND MODERN,

NATURAL AND ARTISTIC;

WITH THE ART OF

WORKING IN HAIR.

ILLUSTRATED BY NUMEROUS DESIGNS.

By Alexanna Speight.

LONDON:
1872.

original title page

Originally published in 1872 with the title:

THE LOCK OF HAIR
ITS HISTORY, ANCIENT AND MODERN
NATURAL AND ARTISTIC
WITH THE ART OF
WORKING IN HAIR
ILLUSTRATED BY NUMEROUS DESIGNS
BY ALEXANNA SPEIGHT
LONDON, 1872

PUBLISHER'S NOTE:

The text of this book is printed unabridged with the exception of :

Page layout which has been modified to reflect page numbering of the plate illustrations.

Correction of text references to illustrations, most of which were in error in the original edition

CONTENTS

Note: Numbers in [ ] designate page numbers of this book. Other page references are from the original edition and are retained for continuity. In the original edition, plates were tipped in, without page numbers.

LACIS
PUBLICATIONS
3163 ADELINE STREET
BERKELEY, CA 94703
© 2004, LACIS
ISBN: 1-891656-60-0

INTRODUCTION

Hair was never quite taken for granted as it embellished the human body as well as the human spirit.

Off the body, hair became an important element of association, being identified with friendship, joy and sorrow.

With the extended forty years of mourning brought about by Queen Victoria's grief during the latter part of the 19th century hair jewelry gained prominence as a reflection of sentiment and mourning and persistent association with sorrow.

Presentation took three major forms:

It was braided in elaborate and decorative open web, flat and round, forms worked on a stool, each group of working strands tensioned by connecting weights. The finished braid was generally fitted with gold fittings and made into bracelets, necklaces, watch bobs and other ornamental objects. *THE ART OF HAIR WORK, HAIR BRAIDING AND JEWELRY OF SENTIMENT by Mark Campbell* originally published in 1875 [Lacis edition 1994] remains the definitive resource for this technique.

The other popular form was that of dimensional flowers and the memorial wreaths, typically representing entire families. Working with wire and the techniques of northern European straw work, these pieces were typically large and designed for wall display. A source for this type of work is *Decorative Straw Craft by Barbara Fitch.*

The more popular placement of hair was in brooches and rings of increasingly larger size. Protected by glass and secured with gold mounts, the high level of precision required for this work enabled the formation of natural, recognizable forms such as flowers, feathers, trees, butterflies, etc. The most important manual for this type of work is this current book *The Lock of Hair*. Alexanna Speight (there remains controversy as to whether a male or female belongs to this name) had a business establishment in London, catering to English royalty at the height of the great mourning era. This manual was intended to encourage the novice to create their own hair devices and thus be insured that substituted hair was not used, which was common with the commercial hair workers. Part II of this book was published, unabridged, under the title *HAIR ORNAMENTS: THE ART OF WORKING IN HAIR* by the National Artistic Hairwork Company (Chicago) in 1887. *LADIES' FANCY WORK*, a resource for all variety of Victorian crafts published an extensive instructional article on this type of work in 1876 which has been reprinted under the title *HAIR WORK & OTHER LADIES' FANCY WORK by Mrs. C.S. Jones & Henry T. Williams.*

All resources referred to are available from this publisher.

LACIS Publisher

PREFACE.

In the following pages, hair will be found to be looked at from two very distinct points of view : first, on the head, and then off the head. In the earlier pages, we have the human hair bearing its part in the ever varying fashions of the day ; at one time flowing in ringlets, at another cropped as closely as shears could cut. Now expanding freely in genuine Tresses, and then tied down in the hideous but undeceiving wig. In this portion of our pages, we hope the reader will find much that will be amusing, and serve to pass away a leisure hour. The second part, however, will explain the main object of the writer. The endeavour is by means of easy explanations and illustrations, to bring the art of working in hair within the reach of every one. It is hoped that the introduction of an agreeable occupation, and one that may serve to while away many long winter evening or summer afternoon, will require no excuse. It may not, however, be out of place to mention, that the Author's attention was first directed to the object of the book by one of those pieces of trade jugglery which will be found described in p. 84. As it appears not to suit the purpose of professional hair workers to work up, in all cases, the materials entrusted to them, they cannot complain if those who would employ them, are taught to dispense with their services, and to become masters of the beautiful art themselves.

THE LOCK OF HAIR.

BY

ALEXANNA SPEIGHT.

WHEN we think or speak of human hair we naturally enough associate it with the human head. The mind recalls the curly locks of youth, dwells upon the flowing tresses or gigantic superstructure of womanhood, or mournfully turns away from the spare and scattered grey covering of old age. But however we may look upon it in admiration or in sorrow, we still connect hairs with heads. There are, however, stories told of people wearing their hair not only on their heads but in their hearts. Valerius Maximus tells us that the heart of Aristomenes, the Messenian, was hairy. A similar story is told of Hermogenes, the Rhetorician, by Cœlius Rhodiginus, and of Leonides, the Spartan, by Plutarch. We are not informed how the hairiness of these evidently hard-hearted men was discovered, and we may well imagine that the

[5]

story did not originate with the individuals themselves. A more likely tale is told by Amatus Lusitanus of a person who had hair upon his tongue. We can quite understand what a rough tongue this gentleman must have had, and how he must have revelled in anything like a difference of opinion with a neighbour. Bundles of hair have been found, it is said, in the muscular parts of beef, and of the human frame, but how they got there, or the purpose they served, having taken up their abode in such apparently unsuitable places we need not stop to enquire.

The mode of wearing the hair seems to have occupied a large share of the attention of good-looking humanity from the very earliest times, and to have been a source of endless disputes between priests and penitents, conquerors and conquered.

Among the Jews the hair was worn long by all except the priests. We can judge what Absolom's hair was when we are told that it weighed as much as two hundred shekels ; and Solomon, Josephus tells us was in the habit of being preceded on grand occasions by forty pages, with their hair powdered with gold dust.

The Jewish priests had their hair cut every fortnight, whilst they were in waiting at the temple.

They used no razors, however, but scissors only. The Nazarites, too, whilst their vow continued, were forbidden to touch their heads with a razor. The Jewish and Grecian ladies gave quite as much of their attention to their hair as do the ladies of our own days, but we doubt whether the results were not more satisfactory.

Perhaps no style of hairdressing for elegance and simplicity equalled that of the Greeks, among whom both men and women gathered the hair up into a kind of knot on the top of the head, often ornamenting it with a grasshopper.

The Jewish women generally wore their hair long, dressed in a variety of ways, and adorned with gold, silver, pearls, and other ornaments. The Jewish men, however, in turn took to wearing their hair cut short, as did the Greeks and Romans, if we are to judge from medals, statues, and other monuments and remains. Indeed the length of the hair seems to have formed, as it does now, one of the principal distinctions in the dress of the sexes.

The Assyrians, we learn, were also very particular with respect to their hair; and as to their beards, let any one look at the Ninevah marbles in the British Museum, and he will easily get some notion of the splendour of those exquisitely plaited and curled appendages.

Egyptian antiquities supply us with much information on the care which that nation bestowed upon their hair and beards. They are said to have shaved their heads and chins, and to have indulged not only in wigs, but in artificial beards. Their kings had their beards interwoven with gold thread, and the beard of a deity is represented in one of their sculptures as being turned up at the end.

On the coins of the Parthian kings, and of Juba, are to be found Egyptian figures with a very odd coiffure, which has been considered by some to have been no more than a peruke of wool. Judging from the figures of Isis, the Egyptian women appear to have had their hair cut square round the neck, something after the manner of those very little girls of our own times, who are too young to have lost simplicity or acquired chignons.

The hair had something to do with matrimony among the Greeks. Our young brides and bridesmaids cover their beauty and tresses with veils on those joyous occasions, and pass through the ordeal unshorn. The Grecian youth and maiden, on the other hand, a few days before the marriage, cut off and consecrated their hair as on offering to their favourite deities. The hair, too, had its uses in mourning. It was customary to hang the hair of the dead on their doors previous to interment, and the mourners not unfrequently tore, cut off, or shaved their own hair, which they laid upon the corpse, or threw into the pile to be consumed along with the body of the relation or friend whose loss they lamented.

It was supposed by the ancients that no one could die until a lock of hair was cut off, and this act they imagined to be performed by the invisible hand of death, or of some messenger from the gods, and the hair thus cut off was supposed to consecrate the dead to the infernal deities, under whose control they were believed to be placed. It was a sort of first fruits which sanctified the whole.

The Chinese still, we are told, distinguish the status of their ladies by the head-dress. From infancy to marriage the girl wears the back part of her hair braided into a tail, and the rest combed over her forehead, and cut into the shape of a crescent. On the day of marriage she wears a sort of crown, covered with tinsel paper, and the following day she adopts the well known tea-pot style. The Chinese widow, instead of the hideous English head-dress, supposed to be indicative of grief, has part of her head shaved, and binds her hair round in a fillet, fastened with many bodkins, some of them expensive. As for the head of the Chinaman, everybody knows what he does with his hair, shaving away all but that solitary tuft on the top, of which he is so proud. Some of our readers may not be aware, however, that the tail, now so much cherished, was originally a mark of their subjection to the Tartars. The origin of the beautiful appendage, however, is without any importance to the mind of the celestial. He thinks it looks well, and that it is not without its seductive influences upon Miss John Chinaman, and what other gratification has ever been needed for any kind of personal adornment.

There were long-haired swells even among our very early forefathers. The ancient Britons were extremely proud of the length and beauty of their hair, and spent no inconsiderable amount of time and trouble in the dressing and adorning their heads. Not contented, too, with the natural colour of their fair or yellow hair, they made use of certain washes, to render it still brighter. One of these washes is said to have been composed of tallow, the ashes of certain vegetables, and lime. Some of these ancient persons carried the fondness for their hair to an almost inconceivable extent, and a story is told of a young warrior, who, having been taken prisoner, and condemned to be beheaded, earnestly requested that no slave might be permitted to touch his long and beautiful hair, and that it might not be stained with his blood. The sad little story reminds one of the last scene in the life of Sir Thomas More, who, on laying his head upon the block, carefully put aside his long beard, asking that it might not be disturbed, as it at least had never offended the king.

Our more immediate predecessors in this country, the Danes and Anglo-Saxons, had quite the same weakness for long hair as the Britons, whom they drove into the mountain fastnesses of the West. They, too, considered flowing locks as one of the greatest beauties and ornaments of their persons, and were at no small pains in dressing them to the greatest possible advantage. Young ladies, before marriage, wore their hair uncovered and untied, and flowing in heart-breaking ringlets over their shoulders; but as soon as husbands were won, the successful tresses were abandoned, as things that had served their purpose, and were without further use. The hair was cut shorter, tied up, and covered by some head-dress or other, according to the prevailing fashion of the time. We are not told whether the flowing locks came back with disconsolate widowhood, but we may at least safely assume that whatever mode of head-dress they adopted as indicating their sorrows and their hopes, the Anglo-Saxon ladies valued their good looks far too much to indulge in weeds such as spoil many a pretty face in these more mournful days of ours. The hair-cutting which thus accompanied matrimony still left remaining, however, much of woman's finest ornament; for to have the hair cut off altogether was considered so great a disgrace that it formed one of the severest punishments inflicted on those women who had been convicted of crime.

In the reigns of those two very unsatisfactory Monarchs—Edgar, the Peaceable, and Ethelred, the Unready—there were Danish soldiers quartered upon the people of England who gave themselves high airs, and were probably looked upon as swells of the purest water. We can judge what they were from the old Danish poem, the death-song of Lodbroc, where we find a "lover of the lady beauteous in his locks." Royalty, too, did its duty, as a leader of fashion, to some purpose, for we find that the locks of king

Canute hung over his shoulders in rich profusion. At all events the young Danes were the beaux of the period, and particularly attentive to the dressing of their hair, which, says a writer, " they combed at least once every day, and thereby captivated the affections of the English ladies."

If we only remember that Astrologers are found to speak of lucky days, for combing the hair a longer interval than a day between each hair-dressing does not seem so improbable as might at first sight appear. It is pleasant, however, to find so easy a road to the hearts of our fair countrywomen, and we shall not be in any way surprised to find the impressionable youths who read these pages devoting unusual attention to their hair, combing it regularly once a day, and securing on all sides the objects of their affections. Let the disconsolate and rejected take fresh hope, and comb themselves into married and happy men with all possible dispatch.

The Danes and Anglo-Saxons seem to have travelled beyond the confines of comb and brush in their search for loveliness in hair, and appear to have gone to the length of colouring it in rather a free way. What would our young lady readers—who aim at and attain these golden locks, which nature in her tender mercy towards the less important sex denied them, but which art supplies—think of sky-blue forehead curls, or a green " follow me lads ?" It is an error to suppose that that arch bigamist of the nursery, " Blue Beard," is the only one who ever indulged in azure, either upon the chin or head. Unless the artists who illustrated some of our ancient chronicles are awful story tellers, striking tints were by no means uncommon in the hair-dressing of the period. Strutt, in speaking of those Anglo-Saxon manuscripts in which the hair and beard are frequently painted blue, says, " In some instances which are not so common the hair is represented of a bright red colour, and in others it is of a green and orange hue. I have no doubt existing in my own mind that arts of some kind were practiced at this period to colour the hair, but whether it was done by tinging or dyeing it with liquids prepared for that purpose, according to the ancient Eastern custom, or by powder of different hues cast into it, agreeably to modern practice, I shall not presume to determine."

In the reigns of Henry III. and Edward I, the swells and dandies of the period wore their hair, as any one may see in pictures illustrating the time, very bushy at the sides, and arranged in enormous curls. Chaucer speaks of the hair of the Young Squire as being curled as if laid in a press, and in the Knight's tale thus describes the fair Emelie—

> Hire yelwe heer was browdid in a tress,
> Behynde hire back a yerde long, I gesse.

In the fourteenth century the ordinary mode of dressing the hair among ladies in this country was by parting it on the forehead, and having it confined at each side of the face in plaits, with a gorget or wimple covering the neck, and drawn up over the chin, strained up each side of the face and then fastened across the forehead, the forehead itself being encircled by a fillet ornamented with jewels. Then over the head was drawn a veil, which fell down upon the shoulders. One may easily see in old pictures of ladies thus attired that the head-dress was by no means an attractive one. Towards the end of the century, however, the style was altered to what appears to have been a very decided improvement. This was a caul, or close cap, made of network, in which the hair was confined round the face. The fronts were filled with different patterns, and the cauls themselves were sometimes made with gold or silver network ornamented with jewels.

With the fifteenth century came in the horned

head-dresses. The side cauls of the Crespine head-dress were always large, and thus the outer edges became elevated above the forehead, so as to form horns. Later in the same century the horned head-dress among ladies of fashion gave way to a still more preposterous style, that of the wired or butterfly head-dress. The hair was drawn into a cap richly orna-mented, and over the cap was extended a veil of quite a superb description. Just as this century was going out bonnets came in, and very remarkable bonnets they must have been, judged by the tiny affairs of our own times. The leading characteristic of the bonnet of the fifteenth century was its long lappets, which formed a kind of angle over the forehead, and hung down on each side. We have not even yet done with the changes of the fifteenth century, for there has still to be mentioned the steeple head-dress, with a long veil hanging down behind, which we can quite imagine was an effective piece of female adorn-ment.

With the sixteenth century came small trim circu-lar caps, then a sort of close cap, which projected for-ward at each side of the face, and often had appended to it a jewelled fillet over the forehead, and a lappet hanging behind. Later on it was not unusual to have the hair brushed back from the temples, a hood having a lappet behind being thrown forward over the top of the head. These fashions, like our modern ones, seem to have been of French origin, for we find a French writer of the period thus speaking of the prevailing folly : — " One manner of spoiling and abusing one's vestments is as to the form, which, as regards women, I consider in four parts. The first is the head, which used to be horned, but is now mitred in these parts of France, * ' * * * and now these mitres are in the shape of chimneys, * * * * and the more beautiful and younger the wearer the higher chimneys they carry." In France during the 18th century the head-dresses of women of rank took the form of mimic frigates, and bunches of artificial fruit or vegetables. It is barely possible that hair-dressing could have attained to a greater height of extravagance than was displayed in the horned style just mentioned. These two cones, or spires, built up on each side of the head, were of such dimensions that a woman who was but a pigmy without her head-dress appeared like a colossus upon putting it on. Monsieur Paradin says, that " these old-fashioned furtanges rose an ell above the head, that they were pointed like steeples, and had long loose pieces of crape fastened to the tops of them, which were curiously fringed and hung down their backs like streamers." There is no saying how high women might not have carried this gothic building had not a famous Monk, Thomas Conecte by name, attacked it with irresistible vigour. This holy man travelled from place to place to preach down the fashion, and succeeded so well in it that the magicians sacrificed their books to the flames. Many of the women threw down their head-dresses in the middle of his sermon, and made a bonfire of them within sight of the pulpit. He was so renowned as well for the sanctity of his life as his manner of preaching, that he had often a congregation of 20,000 people, the men placing themselves on one side of the pulpit and the women on the other, so that to use the similitude of an ingenious writer, they looked like a forest of cedars, with their heads reaching to the clouds. He so warmed and animated the people against this monstrous ornament that it lay under a kind of persecution, and whenever it appeared in public it was pelted down by the rabble, who flung stones at the persons that wore it.

But notwithstanding that this prodigy vanished while the preacher was present, it began to appear again some months after his departure, or, to give it in Mons. Paradin's own words, " the women that, like snails in a fright, had drawn in their horns, shot them out again as soon as the danger was over." The same extravagance of women's head-dresses in that age is taken notice of by Mons. D'Argentié, in the History of Bretagne, and by other historians.

However they may have afterwards declined, the head-dresses of English ladies, about a hundred years ago rose to something like a marvellous height. They towered three feet above their heads, and lest these ponderous arrangements should be disturbed, the unhappy wearers not unfrequently slept in chairs instead of going to bed. Theatrical managers complained with some reason that the large head-dresses in the front rows prevented those behind from seeing the performances. In a caricature of the period, called "A New Opera Glass, for 1777," a gentleman is represented as using one of the great curls at the side of a lady's head as an opera glass, and below is written—

> Behold how Jemmy treats the fair,
> And makes a telescope of hair ;
> How will this suit high-headed lasses,
> If curls are turned to optic glasses ?"

We find a singular instance of the way fashions repeat themselves in the assault made upon the style of hair-dressing prevailing upwards of a hundred and fifty years ago. Public writers then as now attacked the extravagance with which ladies built up their own or other peoples tresses. " Within my own memory," says one who lived and wrote in the year 1711, " I have known a lady's head-dress to rise and fall above thirty degrees. About ten years ago it shot up to a very great height, insomuch that the female part of our species were much taller than the men. The women were of such an enormous stature, that we appeared as grasshoppers before them. At present the whole sex is in a manner dwarfed and shrunk into a race of beauties that seems almost another species. I remember several ladies who were once near seven feet high, and at present want some inches of five ; how they came to be thus curtailed I cannot learn, whether the whole sex be at present under any penance which we know nothing of, or whether they have cast their head-dresses in order to surprise us with something in that kind which shall be entirely new, or whether some of the tallest of the sex, being too cunning for the rest, have contrived this method to make themselves appear sizeable, is still a secret ; though I find most are of opinion they are at present like trees new lopped and pruned, that will certainly sprout up and flourish with greater heads than before.

For my own part I do not love to be insulted by women who are taller than myself. I admire the sex much more in their present humiliation, which has reduced them to their natural dimensions, than when they had extended their persons, and lengthened themselves out into formidable and gigantic figures. I am not for adding to the beautiful edifices of nature, nor for raising any whimsical superstructure upon her plans. I must, therefore, repeat it, that I am highly pleased with the coiffure now in fashion, and think it shows the good sense which at present very much reigns amongst the valuable part of the sex. One may observe that women in all ages have taken more pains than men to adorn the outside of their heads, and indeed I very much admire those female architects who raise such wonderful structures out of ribbons, lace, and wire, and wonder they have not yet been re-warded for their respective inventions. It is certain that there has been as many orders in these kinds of building as in those which have been made of marble. Sometimes they rise in the shape of a pyramid; sometimes like a tower; sometimes like a steeple. In Juvenal's time the building grew by several orders and stories, as he humourously described it—

> With curls on curls they build her head before,
> And mount it with a formidable tower,—
> A giantess she seems, but look behind,
> And then she dwindles to the pygmy kind.

The writer then goes on to give some advice, which is not only good, but applicable to this as to that time. " I could desire," he says, " the fair sex to consider how impossible it is for them to add anything that can be ornamental to what is already the master-piece of nature. The head has the most beautiful appearance, as well as the highest station, in the human figure. Nature has laid out all her art in beautifying the face: she has touched it with vermillion, planted in it a double row of ivory, made it the seat of smiles and blushes, lighted it up and enlivened it with the brightness of the eyes, hung it on each side with curious organs of sense, given it airs and graces that cannot be described, and surrounded it with such a glowing shade of hair, as sets all its beauties in the most agreeable light ; in short she seems to have designed the head as the cupola to the most glorious of her works, and when we load it with such a pile of supernumerary ornaments we destroy the symmetry of the human figure, and foolishly contrive to call off the eye from great and real beauties to childish geegaws, ribbons, and bruc lace."

Hear, too, what Pope sings of one of woman's brightest charms :—

> This nymph, to the destruction of mankind,
> Nourished two locks, which graceful hung behind
> In equal curls, and well conspired to deck
> With shining ringlets the smooth ivory neck.
> Love in these labrynths his slaves detains,
> And mighty hearts are held in slender chains.
> With hairy springes we the birds betray,
> Slight lines of hair surprise the finny prey;
> Fair tresses Man's imperial race insnare,
> And beauty draws us with a single hair.
>   The adventurous baron the bright locks admired ;
> He saw, he wished, and to the prize aspired.
> Resolved to win, he meditates the way,
> By force to ravish, or by fraud betray ;
> For when success a lover's toil attends
> Few ask if fraud or force attained his ends.
>
>   *   *   *   *   *
>
> And see through all things with his half-shut eyes,
> Sent up in vapors to the Baron's brain
> New stratagems, the radiant Lock to gain.
> Ah, cease, rash youth! desist, ere 'tis too late,
> Fear the just gods, and think of Scilla's fate !
> Changed to a bird, and sent to flit in air,
> She dearly pays for Nisus' injured hair !
>   But when to mischief mortals bend their will,
> How soon they find fit instruments of ill !
> Just then Clarissa drew, with tempting grace,
> A two-edged weapon from her shining case :
> So ladies in romance assist their knight,
> Present the spear, and arm him for the fight.
> He takes the gift with reverence, and extends
> The little engine on his fingers' ends ;
> This just behind Belinda's neck he spread,
> As o'er the fragrant steam she bends her head.
> Swift to the Lock a thousand sprites repair,
> A thousand wings, by turns, blow back the hair ;

And thrice they twitch'd the diamond in her ear;
Thrice she look'd back, and thrice the foe drew near.
Just in that instant anxious Ariel sought
The close recesses of a virgin's thought:
As on the nosegay in her breast reclined,
He watch'd the ideas rising in her mind,
Sudden he view'd, in spite of all her art,
An earthly lover lurking at her heart.
Amazed, confused, he found his power expired,
Resign'd to fate, and with a sigh retired.

The Peer now spreads the glittering forfex wide,
To inclose the Lock; now joins it, to divide.
Even then, before the fatal engine closed,
A wretched sylph too fondly interposed;
Fate urged the shears, and cut the sylph in twain,
(But airy substance soon unites again;)
The meeting points the sacred hair dissever
From the fair head, for ever, and for ever!

Then flashed the living lightning from her eyes,
And screams of horror rend the affrighted skies;
Not louder shrieks to pitying heaven are cast,
When husbands, or when lap-dogs, breathe their last
Or when rich China vessels, fallen from high,
In glittering dust, and painted fragments lie!

Let wreaths of triumph now my temples twine,
(The victor cried,) the glorious prize is mine!
While fish in streams, or birds delight in air,
Or in a coach-and-six the British fair,
As long as Atalantis shall be read,
Or the small pillow grace a lady's bed,
While visits shall be paid on solemn days,
When numerous wax-lights in bright order blaze,
While nymphs take treats, or assignations give,
So long my honour, name, and praise shall live!
What time would spare, from steel receives its date,
And monuments, like men, submit to fate!
Steel could the labour of the gods destroy,
And strike to dust the imperial towers of Troy;
Steel could the works of mortal pride confound,
And hew triumphal arches to the ground.
What wonder then, fair nymph! thy hairs should feel
The conquering force of unresisted steel?

[24]

The following skit, written in August, 1776, upon the " modern belle," gives rather an amusing account of how the heads of the ladies of the day appeared. We will not say to what extent the verses would need alteration to meet the ladies of our own times :—

Muse begin the comic lay,
Sing the female of to-day,
Yet to person be confined,
Nor dare meddle with her mind,
Lest the strange investigation
Cause thee trouble and vexation,
'Twere to seek, alas a-day,
Needles in a stack of hay.
Void of talents, sense, and art,
Dress is now her better part ;
Sing her daubed with white and red,
Sing her large terrific head ;
Nor the many things disguise
That produce its mighty size ;
And let nothing be forgot,
Carrots, turnips, and what not :
Curls and cushions for imprimus,
Wool and powder for the finis ;
Lace and lappets many a flag—
Many a party-coloured rag—
Pendant from the head behind,
Floats and wantons in the wind,
Many a gem, and many a feather,
Choice fanago all together,
By whose wood and wire assistance,
(Formidable at a distance,
As the elephants of yore
A famed Queen to battle bore,)
They with honour and surprise
Strike the poor beholder's eyes,
What a quantity of brain
Must he think such heads contain,

Though it prove a false alarm,
Feather brains can do no harm,
Hats that only show the chin,
And the mouth's bewitching grin,
As intended for a shield
To the caput thus concealed;
Surely 'tis an useful art
Well to guard the weakest part.
Shoes that buckle at the toe,
Gowns that o'er the pavement flow,
Or festooned on either side,
With two yellow ribbons tied,
While a peak, like pigeon's rump,
Shows behind she's not too plump,
Heels that bear the precious charge,
More diminutive than large;
Slight and brittle, apt to break,
Of the true Italian make,
For women of *bon ton*, observe ye,
Like sugar-loaves turned topsy turvy,
As their heaviest part 's a top
Rest upon a feeble prop,
And, that all mankind may know it,
Toss about their heads and show it!

It may occur to some of our readers to enquire, amidst all this hair-dressing, whence came the artists? The art, at least as practiced in these days, seems like most of our little elegancies, to have come to us from France. In the " Gentleman's Magazine " we find, just nearly a century ago, a characteristic British growl about a school of hair-dressers then at work in Paris. A " wanderer" thus writes to Sylvanus Urban:—" Paris, June 12.—Mr. Urban, among the oddities which present themselves every minute to the eyes of a stranger in the fluttering city, I have been highly entertained with one in particular, i.e., the academy for teaching the art of female hair-dressing according to the present high *gout*. In my walks I have seen several of these, where a large room with its contents is laid open to public view, and wherein you see a great number of the dirtiest female drabs the streets afford, hired to sit (as we phrase it) not for their pictures, but their patience, and to have their heads and their hair twisted and turned about in various forms, according to the taste of the operator. Some of these ladies in high dress have been so wonderfully picturesque that I have been more than once in danger of breaking a blood-vessel; nor is it less entertaining to observe with what astonishment and delight some of them look into the glass under their elegant coiffeure. Yet I must confess that I have seen others who have exhibited well-bred faces, looked full as like women of fashion as their betters, a look which no dress can give to a low educated woman of our nation. When a head is finished the whole chamber of artists examine the workmanship, and after each has given his opinion the pyramid is thrown down and re-erected by some other student. Before I have well recovered from the soarness and a fit of coughing, which laughing is apt to produce on me, my eyes are struck with two golden angels sounding trumpets, and which, in the joint actions of flying and walking, support their trumpets with one hand, each holding a well-combed peruque with the other. By this you will perceive, Mr. Urban, that the head and hair are the two main objects of a Frenchwoman's attention." Far exceeding the most brilliant efforts of the academy, however, were the promises held out by a Siberian hair-dresser to the ladies of London. This ingenious person, Iwan Peter Alexis Knoutschoff-schlerwitz, in offering his services to the ladies in the important art of hair-dressing, engages to execute it in a manner peculiar to himself, rejecting the use of black pins, hair cushions, and the like cumbersome materials, so dangerous in their effects. He avoids the use of a great many abominations, which he enumerates, but which we abstain from mentioning. Instead of these he fills the hollows of the hair with soft aromatic herbs, which " prevent the disagreeable effect of that perspiration now so generally complained of." He dresses hair in every mode, and engages to make any lady's head appear like the head of a lion, a wolf, a tiger, a bear, a fox, or any exotic beast which she would choose to resemble. He does not, however, confine himself to beasts, for to any body who happened to prefer the form of a peacock, a swan, a goose, a Friesland hen, or any other bird, he engaged to give a perfect likeness. He also offered to give any colour to the hair that a lady might judge most suitable to her complexion, for as every single hair is an hollow tube, though imperceptible to the naked eye, he, by injecting a certain liquid, communicated the finest shades, and rendered the use of powder unnecessary, thereby effecting, as a wag of the day observes, a great saving in bread corn. Ladies whose hair indicated the time of life which they wished to conceal could be secretly and safely accommodated by this interesting Siberian. He could change their locks into a fine chesnut, blue, crimson, or green, according to the mode which might generally prevail. The advantages of Iwan Knoutscoffschlerwitz did not end here—for his wife was a milliner, and it was hoped that her own merit, added to that of her being a foreigner, would engage the favour of the ladies. She made caps of any size from twenty inches to three feet high, which being composed of certain elastic springs, gave way when a lady went into her coach or chair, without discomposing the form, as it rose immediately to its original height when the lady got out of her coach. She had then also substituted in the place of radishes and other garden stuff the ornaments of the period—aromatic spices—which, independent of the decoration, had other admirable effects. To meet the fluctuations of fashions Mrs. Knoutschoffschlerwitz was prepared for any change, and had made some pattern caps of a low moderate size, which did not take the head out of its proportion, but preserved its due equality to the rest of the human form. To these caps she had given an air of softness that added a delicacy to the features of the fair, freeing them from that ferocity which in the then existing mode the other sex so much complained of. She had already had the honour of dressing a few ladies in that taste who she had the pleasure to find had been particularly admired by the men, but as she did not presume to attempt stemming the torrent of fashion, she was ready to supply all those ladies who were still desirous of carrying their heads high, with caps of any dimensions. She had brought over a number of live ostriches, peacocks, &c., that ladies who meant to persist in the use of feathers, though the fashion was then exploded in Siberia, and throughout all Russia, might be accommodated to their taste; and she engaged to ingraft them with natural hair, rendering the operation the least painful. In like manner gentlemen whose skulls were from age become rather a little too bare, and who yet could not submit to the Gothic taste of covering them with wigs, might have natural hair inserted in as sure and easy a manner as they were supplied with teeth, and which would hold for months without renewal; and any lady or gentleman in this predicament might be served by the year on very moderate terms.

The sudden change of hair from all colours into the brightest golden, which astonished and perplexed the male portion of the population some few years since, and required the father to be indeed a wise one who could know his own child when changed from a flashing Brunette into a languishing Blonde, was after all but the restoration of a very ancient art, and it really is very questionable whether the glorious golden hues of bright yellow hair have not after all a natural and superior attractiveness, which would account for the constant efforts which one after another are seen repeating themselves, to attain through science what nature has denied. Fair haired women seem to have been the favourites of painters and poets. Among the old Venetian Masters golden tresses are to be seen every where, and it is a remarkable fact that in any large collection of works of the Old Masters there is a very singular absence of dark heads. It is possible that the fashion of golden hair prevailed to such an extent that the painters did no more than reproduce, as there is little doubt the Venetian painters did, the beauties by whom they were surrounded. Shakespeare, who scarcely ever mentions black hair throughout his entire plays, speaks in the Merchant of Venice of " Sunny locks on her temples like golden fleece."

The art of hair-dyeing seems to have been not unknown among the Greeks, for have we not the story of the Sculptor Miron, who at the ripe age of seventy fell in love with Lais, and after he had been rejected appeared next day with his hoary locks dyed black, and renewed his suit, but only again to be repulsed. " How can I," said Lais, " grant thee to-day what I refused to thy father yesterday. Most of our readers will we are sure think with us, that she treated the old gentleman as he deserved.

That the art was also well known to the Romans is beyond all question. They not unfrequently dyed their hair black, and for this purpose used a liquid dye prepared from leeches, that had been left for sixty days to putrify. The yellow tint, however, at least in later years, became the favourite one. The Roman ladies seem to have adopted a somewhat similar means for the purpose of securing golden tresses. They used a soap called from Mallium in Germany, Malliac balls, composed of goats fat and ashes; and Galen tells us that in his time some ladies attempted to obtain the golden tint by the use of saffron, while others suffered much from headaches contracted by standing bareheaded in the sun, for the purpose of acquiring the coveted colour. Others more sensible boldly removed their dark hair, and replaced it by a wig of the fashionable colour; and we may judge how general this practice had become when we find statues and busts in the Vatican and elsewhere actually wearing marble wigs. This yellow dying is handed down to us by the pens of Ovid and Catullus, and the pencils of Titian and Giorgione. When Venice was Queen of the Adriatic golden hair was irresistably fashionable. If we were to judge from the portraits and historical masterpieces of the Venetian painters we should expect to find Venice a paradise of *Blondes* and yet it is the *Brunettes* who predominated—the Blonde was a mere work of art. Cesare Vicillio, writing in 1589, thus pictures a fair Venetian, with her dripping head exposed to the

sun :—" The houses of Venice,' he writes, " are
commonly crowned with little constructions in wood,
resembling a turret without a roof. On the ground
these lodges or boxes are formed of masonry, floored
like, what are called terazzi at Florence and Naples,
and covered with a cement of sand and lime to
protect them from the rain. It is in these that the
Venetian women may be seen as often, and indeed
oftener, than in their chambers ; it is there that with
their heads exposed to the full ardour of the sun
during whole days they strain every nerve to augment
their charms, as if they needed it,—as if the constant
use of so many methods known to all did not expose
their natural beauty to pass for no better than
artificial. During the hours when the sun darts its
most vertical and scorching rays they repair to these
boxes and condemn themselves to broil in them
unattended. Seated there they keep on wetting their
hair with a sponge dipped in some Elixir of Youth,
prepared with their own hands or purchased. They
moisten their hair afresh as fast as it is dried by the
sun, and it is by the unceasing renewal of this operation that they become what you see them—*Blondes.*
When engaged in it they throw over their ordinary
dress a *peignoir*, or dressing gown, of the finest white

silk, which they call a *Schia-ronetto*. They wear on
their heads a straw hat without a crown, so that the
hair drawn through the opening may be spread upon
the borders; this hat, doing double duty as a drying-
line for the hair and a parasol to protect the neck and
face, was called *Solana*. In winter, or when the sun
failed, they wetted and dried their hair before a fire."

Far be it from us to enquire too minutely into the
means by which our fair ladies of England manage
the transformation of raven locks into golden—we
devoutly hope, however, that the English Villas,
detached or semi-detached, contain no torture turrets
like those frequented by the Dames of Venice. If we
are wrong, how much they must have suffered for the
sake of those who are but half sensible of changing
charms. In the times we speak of very eminent
physicians indeed were not above ministering to
female vanity: Dr. Marinello, of Modenna, the author
of a " Light of Apothicaries, and Treasure of Hero-
borists" in 1562, published as a Treatise upon the
Adornment of Women. To say that the ladies swore
by this book would be a shocking impropriety; if
they did not swear by it, however, they thoroughly
believed as they ought to have done in a writer who thus
gallantly concludes his book of receipts : " Permit

me," writes the Doctor, "to remind you honoured and honourable ladies that the application of so many colours to your hair may strike a chill into the head like the shock of a shower-bath, that it affects and penetrates, and, what is worse, may entail divers grave maladies and infirmities; therefore I should advise you to take all possible precautions. For example, mix doses of musk amber, and other heating and stimulating ingredients, with your ungents and elixirs. What may not otherwise happen even as regards the colour your hair may turn out rough, coarse, and altogether changed for the worse, a disaster which you will avoid if you take care to add to your compositions things fit to soften them—things which I have enumerated in another place. We frequently see the hair affected in its essentials, or at its roots grow weak and fall off, and the complexion destroyed, through the use of so many injurious liquids and decoctions.—Recur for the first case to oil of violet, and for the second to olive oil warm—your complexion will immediately recover its most becoming tints. In all and each of these little things and ways sweet and honourable ladies have infinite prudence, so as to avoid the self-reproach of the terrible evils that may ensue."

It would be impertinent in us to observe upon the good advice thus affectionately conveyed by the old Doctor, but we would re-echo his warning against the use of the ungents and elixirs, even when accompanied by the warming drugs. Another prescription that of Alexis, of Piedmont, for making "heare as yelow as golde," is worth quoting :—" Take the ryne or the scrappynges of rubarbe, and steepe it in white wyne, or in clear lye, and after you have washed your head with it you shall weate your heares with a sponge, or some other clothe, and lette them drye by the fyre, or in the sunne. After this weate them and drye them agayne, for the oftener you dooe the fairer they will be, without hurting your head anyething at all." Lest any of our readers should feel disposed to avail themselves of this prescription, we think it is well to warn them that we know nothing whatever as to its efficacy in " makeying their heare fairer the oftener they dooe it," but as to the "sunne dryeing or fyre dryeing" we are convinced that it, instead of not hurting their heads " anyething at all," would be found to be not only injurious but unpleasant.

Then who has not heard of the sad fate of Mr. Tittlebat Titmouse, the hero of " Ten Thousand a Year," who, wishing to modify an exceedingly red head of hair, wasted his substance upon a bottle having a very long name, rose next morning with his locks pea green, and was compelled to subdue the brilliancy of the result to something like a neutral tint by the aid of a pair of blacking brushes. If the fate of Titmouse is not warning enough, remember Theodore Hooks, Major : that officer, finding his hair getting thin and grey, rubbed his head with an infallible specific that had been recommended to him, and kept, as directed, his night cap on for twenty-four hours ; on at length removing the night cap he was startled by its close resemblance to a crow's nest—the whole of his hair had come off in it.

Hair-dressing and shaving seem to be such kindred arts that one feels oneself entitled to look upon them as two branches of the same profession ; but at what time the useful and economical art of easy shaving was first introduced into this country we cannot venture to say. Hair-curling must have been a practice of some antiquity, and is said to have been extensively used among the Phrygians and Sybarites. The Armenians wore their hair twisted into the form of a mitre. The Persians wore their hair curled, but long and flowing ; whilst the Arabians aimed at a totally opposite style, and had their hair cut upon the crown of the head ; but the date at which the hireling razor first appeared we are not prepared to determine. We get at this fact, however, that the Ancient Britons and their neighbours the Gauls did something in the way of shaving. So far, however, from making anything like a clean sweep of the ample beards with which, we have little doubt, nature endowed them, they contented themselves with a shaven chin, and indulged in moustaches of great size and beauty no doubt, but of very inconvenient length. Still, however involved in obscurity the art may be, the barbers and hair-dressers of that period can be traced back as very ancient and highly respectable operators. If there be any who doubt we would remind them that the calling was one which, at an early period of our history, was followed by very distinguished persons indeed. In the eighth century it was, we are told, the custom of people of quality to have their children's hair cut for the first time by some distinguished person, whom they held in high respect and esteem, and who by virtue of the ceremony acquired something of the position of a spiritual parent, or god-father. This practice, too, would seem to go back to a still greater antiquity, for we learn that Constantine the Great sent to the Pope the hair of his son

Heraclius, as a token of his desire that he should become his adopted father. It not unfrequently happened, also, when Monks were shorn, that the first lock was cut off by the King, or some great person.

The length of the hair was, from very early times, considered a sign of subjection. Among the Grecian states, whatever might be the fashion of the hair among the freemen, slaves were forbidden to imitate it. The hair of the slaves was always cut in a particular manner, which they abandoned as soon as they obtained their freedom. Julius Cæsar, on subduing the Gauls, compelled them to cut their hair as a token of submission. Among these people it was long considered a distinguished honour to have long hair: indeed, hence came the appellation *Gallia Comata*.

Dandyism, as well as superiority of status had also, we may well surmise, something to do with the wearing of long hair by the dominant classes. Martial, in describing the Roman swell, thus writes :—

> A beau is one who with the nicest care,
> In parted locks divides his curling hair;
> One who with balm and Cinnamon smells sweet,
> Whose humming lips some Spanish air repeat.

It was doubtless with a view to the display of

submission we have mentioned that those who afterwards left the world, and went to pass their days in cloisters, had their hair shaven off, as a token of their perpetual subjection to their superiors, and of their abandonment of all earthly ornaments.

As may be readily imagined, with the passion for long hair, grew up in very primitive times indeed, recipes for promoting a luxuriant growth, more or less efficacious, and more or less believed in. Indeed the art of hair cultivation, which is to be seen so gracefully advertised in these days, does not seem to be quite so modern an invention as from its very qualified success one would imagine it to be. Our ancient friends, the Ancient Britons, seem to have been before us in this as in every thing else. They aimed at thick and luxuriant hair, and employed various arts to obtain what they regarded, not only as a great beauty, but as a mark of dignity and nobility of birth. Dio tells us that the ever famous Boadicia, Queen of the Iceni, had long hair flowing over her shoulders, and reaching down below the middle of her back.

Among the Royal family of France it was for a long time, Gregory of Tours tells us, a peculiar mark and privilege of Kings and Princes of the blood to wear long hair. Whilst these distinguished personages wore their hair curled and dressed with all the art of the day, the common folk whom they ruled were polled and cut round in token of inferiority and obedience. We are told also that there were degrees even in this cropping, the closeness of the cut graduating downwards, according to the different qualities and conditions of the liege subjects, from the Prince who indulged in the largest tresses which nature gave him, down to the villain, who was cropped short. It is as well to mention here that the cropped villain of those days was not necessarily so bad a character as the cropped villain of these : one was the mark of grade only, the other is the sign of the county prison.

French Princes had to be almost as careful of their hair as of their heads, for to cut off the hair of a son of France under the first race of Kings declared the shorn Prince excluded from the right of succeeding to the Crown, and reduced him to the condition of an ordinary subject. The scissors having so important an effect upon French succession, we cannot be surprised to find the heads and hairs of the early Kings of France giving a good deal of occupation to the ancient historians and the antiquarians of that country. These writers have been singularly exact in recording the honours of their Sovereigns in this respect. They tell us that Charlemagne wore his hair very short; his son much shorter; and Charles the Bald, as his surname indicates, none at all.

The Clergy seem, from a very early period, to have waged determined and persistent war against those professing Christianity who indulged in long hair. In the progress of the Christian faith the parade of long hair gradually became more and more obnoxious, as something utterly inconsistent with the profession of those who bore the cross, and we consequently find almost innumerable injunctions and canons against the fashion. It is commonly supposed that Pope Anicetus was the first who forbade the Clergy to wear long hair. The Decree in which the prohibition appears is, however, of much later date than this Pope. In the Churches of the East the wearing of long hair is said to have been forbidden at a much earlier period, whilst, according to Isidore, the Clerical tonsure is even of Apostolic institution.

There is a Canon of the year 1096 still extant, which gives a remarkable proof of the odium in which long hair was then held. Such as offended against the orders of the Church in this respect were to be excluded from its privileges whilst living, and were not to be prayed for when dead. Then there is the furious declaration of Luitprand against the Emperor Phocas, for wearing long hair after the manner of the Emperors of the East. These were days in which the occupants of the Holy See spoke in firmer tones than the *Non-possumus* of the Pio Nono of our days. The custom of wearing long hair among the Emperors of the East was, however, not without one noteworthy exception. Theophilas enjoined all his subjects to shave their heads, but the fact that this potentate was himself as bald as a badger accounts for his superiority to fashion.

Another Prince, Mausolus, King of Caria, the same Monarch to whose memory Artemisia erected the celebrated tomb, also ordered a universal shave among his subjects, but with a more reasonable motive. The King being badly in want of money had a large quantity of wigs manufactured, and these he compelled his shorn subjects to buy at his own price to recruit his exhausted treasury.

The Anglo-Saxon Clergy, both secular and regular, were obliged to keep themselves distinguished from the laity by shaving the crowns of their heads, and keeping their hair cut short; and several Canons were published against their concealing their tonsure or allowing their hair to grow long. The shape of the tonsure was the subject of long and violent debates between the English Clergy on the one hand and those of the Picts and Scots on the other. Amongst the former it was circular, whilst the Picts and Scots had it only semicircular. Not only, however, did the Divines quarrel about the shape of the disfigurement, but some, resisting authority, objected to it altogether.

The Norman Priests seem to have been as insubordinate in this respect as they were in everything else connected with luxury. Fabian, the Chronicler, writing at the time of William the Conqueror, says, "At this time the Priests used bushed and braided heads, long-tailed gowns, and blasyn clothes shinying, and golden girdles, and rode with gilt spurs, using of divers other enormities." In fact so eminently esteemed an ornament was long and flowing hair, and such an act of mortification and self-denial was the Clerical tonsure considered, that many less insubordinate among the Priests submitted to it with great reluctance, and endeavoured as much as possible to conceal it. Those among the Clergy who affected the reputation of superior sanctity inveighed with intense bitterness against the long hair of the laity, and laboured earnestly and incessantly to induce them to cut it short, in imitation of the clergy. The famous St. Wulstan, Bishop of Worcester, who declaiming with great vehemence against luxury of all kinds, attacked that of long hair as the most criminal and most universal. The old Chronicler, William of Malmesbury, who writes the Life of this Saint, says, " The English were very vicious in their manners, and plunged into luxury through the long peace which they had enjoyed, in the reign of Edward the Confessor. The Holy Prelate, Wulstan, reproved the wicked of all ranks with great boldness, but he rebuked those with the greatest severity who were proud of their long hair. When any of these vain people bowed their heads before him to receive his blessing, before he gave it he cut a lock of their hair with a little sharp knife, which he carried about him for that purpose, and commanded them, by way of penance for their sins, to cut all the rest of their hair in the same way. If any of them refused to comply with this command he denounced the most dreadful judgments upon them, reproached them for their effeminacy, and foretold that as they imitated women in the length of their hair, they wonld imitate them in their cowardice when their country was invaded, which was accomplished at the landing of the Normans." However sanctified this Saint may have been, he was at all events eminently disagreeable, and if he lived now would be looked upon as a very provoking sort of old man. We must not blame St. Wulstan, however, as he did no more than represent the prevailing Clerical opinion of the day, which was one by no means confined to Anglo-Saxon Priests. After the Conquest the wearing of long hair continued to be a topic of declamation among the Clergy, who even went so far as to represent it as one of the greatest crimes, and a most certain mark of reprobation. Anselm, the Archbishop of Canterbury, even went the length of pronouncing sentence of excommunication against all who wore long hair, and he seems to have been very much commended for his pious zeal. One of the most successful crusaders against the fashion, however, was Serlo, a Norman Bishop, who acquired an undying reputation for a sermon which he preached before Henry I. against long and curled hair. At the time when this Monarch was spending English blood and money, and at the expense of both was earning glory in that old Normandy, which, perhaps, it might have been quite as well if his forefathers had never left, the wearing of long hair was a fashionable vice. The Bishop preached with such eloquence against the fashion, that the King and all his courtiers at once consented to submit to the shears the flowing locks of which they had been so vain. The Bishop was far too prudent to allow vanity any time to re-assert its sway. He came provided, and immediately pulled out a pair of scissors from his sleeve, and performed the operation with his own hand.

There is another instance of similar self-denial, but attended with less happy results. Louis VII. submitted to Clerical exhortations as to the impiety of long hair, and at the instigation of his Bishops had both his hair and beard shaved. His shorn appearance, however, was so dismal, and his Consort Queen Eleanor was so shocked at it, that she obtained a divorce and left him.

King Henry I. went even beyond the shaving—he issued an Edict for the suppression of the prevailing folly. Fashion, however, will re-assert itself, and consequently we very soon find long hair still the rage. In the succeeding reign of Stephen it again received a check, but the cropping was of short duration, as scarcely a year elapsed before people returned to their old follies, and those who set up for being courtiers allowed their hair to grow to such a length that they resembled women rather than men.

About twenty-five years after the shearing of King Henry we find the prevailing fondness for long hair so powerful, that it required a still more remarkable check. It is as well to describe this incident in the words of the contemporary historian :—" An event happened in the year 1129 which seemed very wonderful to our young gallants, who, forgetting that they were men, had transformed themselves into women, by the length of their hair. A certain Knight, who was very proud of his luxuriant hair, dreamed that a person suffocated him with its curls. As soon as he awoke from his sleep he cut his hair to a decent length. The report of this spread over all England, and almost all the Knights reduced their hair to the proper standard. But this reformation was not of long continuance, for in less than a year all those who wished to appear fashionable returned to their former wickedness, and contended with the ladies in length of hair. Those to whom nature had denied that ornament supplied the defect by art."

In the time of the Stuarts we had long hair, with love-locks and heart-breakers. In the reign of James I. the Monarch introduced a new curl, which hung on the left side, and was considerably longer than the rest of the hair. This was the love-lock, and a very troublesome lock it was. In the reign of Charles II. the ladies of the day introduced a long lock of hair— a sort of companion to the love-lock—called " the heart-breaker," and there is little doubt that the heart-breaker was very efficacious and very mischievous. Political parties during the civil wars were far more easily distinguishable than they are in the present evenly flowing times, and a man's party could as readily be determined by his hair as by his speeches.

The Puritans wore their hair so short as scarcely to cover the ears, thus marking their sense of " the loathesomeness of long hair." The Cavaliers, on the other hand, left their locks to flow as long as nature would let them, and where nature would not let them flow at all, they fell back upon the friendly offices of the wig-maker.

It would take pages to enumerate the treatises and essays written upon the lawfulness of wearing long hair. In 1650 there was quite a learned discussion upon the subject, between a Professor of Utrecht, and a Divine named Reeves: both these distinguished persons, we may well believe, wasted a great deal of time and paper in maintaining their opposite views. We have little doubt that neither persuaded the other, and that to the end of their valuable lives the Professor continued to maintain that long hair was unlawful, and the Divine that it was not. These discussions acquired considerable dimensions during the civil wars, for the Puritans attacked both love-locks and long hair with as much virulence as the Clergy had displayed in earlier times. The Author of " The Loathesomeness of Long Haire" has no mercy upon love-locks. " Some men," says he, " have long locks at their ears, as if they had four ears, or were prick-eared. Some have a little long lock before only, hanging down to their noses, like the taile of a weasall, every man being made a fool at the barber's pleasure, or making a foole of the barber for having to make him such a foole." And a Poet of the day thus satirizes the wearing of love-locks :—

> A long love-lock on his left shoulder plight,
> Like to a woman's hair, well showed a woman's sprite.

It is but fair, however, to look at the unattractive-ness of short hair from the Cavalier's point of view. A Song of 1641, called " The Character of a Round-head," thus begins :—

> What creature's this, with his short hairs,
> His little head and huge long ears,
> That this new faith hath founded ?
> The Puritans were never such,
> The Saints themselves had ne'er so much—
> Oh ! such a knave's a Roundhead !

In an old Play of about the same time the Round-heads are spoken of as—

> The Zealous of the land,
> With little hair, and little or no band.

Among the Registers of the Stationers' Company we find under date 1592-3, *Tertio die Februarii*, that "John Wolffe entered for his copie 'A Defence of Shorte Haire.'" We have not looked at the "copie," but we may take it for granted that it fairly represents the controversy then prevailing between the Puritans and their opponents.

It may occur to some of our readers to enquire how, when long hair was the rage, and was fought over in the manner we have described, it fared with those who wished to be in the fashion, and had been denied by nature the possession of those tresses which folly loved and religion anathematized. The answer is easy. They did as they do now: when nature failed them they consulted art. In a word, they wore wigs; and no doubt in this we may trace the origin of wigs, both ancient and modern, for once make long hair the fashion the wig becomes a necessity.

There is no saying of what antiquity the art of hair-dressing can boast: long before lockets were thought of by men, or watch chains entered into the imagination of women, there were artists in hair to be found pursuing their ingenious, if deceptive, calling. The lovely chignon may be modern, the hideous front may be able to claim no nearer associations with past ages than that which exists between itself and its venerable owner ; but wigs have from very early ages been favourably regarded by coquettish humanity. When the world was very young indeed, and took to wig-wearing, it is supposed that these aids to personal beauty were painted hair glued together. In an account given of a wig said to have been worn by a Roman Emperor, it is described as powdered with gold, and oiled and perfumed in such a way as to make the gold adhere. The art must, however, have made rapid strides. In the British Museum is to be seen a wig found at Thebes, in the Temple of Isis, which is a marvel as a work of art. It is of great size; each ringlet is preserved with nicety, and would seem to indicate that the ancient wig-makers could do what their degenerate successors in these days are said to be unable to accomplish, i.e., preserve the curl in the hair.

The introduction of wigs into England is said to date from the time of King Stephen, and like many another contrivance they seem, as we have said, originally to have served to aid nature in the pursuit of fashion. It was the thing to wear long hair, and those who would live in the world as the world lived must supply nature's wants by the hair-dresser's art. There were enlightened men in even the darkest ages, and, as we may readily suppose, long wigs were attacked with as much vigour as ever wasted itself upon long hair. But when did not either folly or fashion come off best in any struggle they ever entered upon? Wigs were written against and railed at, but without effect; when they did give way it was not to the attacks that had been directed against them, but to one of those changes of fashion which are constantly recurring, and which are at the time perfectly irresistible. Those who wear wigs necessarily wear other people's hair, but an inquiry as to who were the original owners is often one that had quite as well be left unanswered. If people will wear the tresses of others they will do well to rest quiet with an easy faith, and whilst rejoicing in all the attractions they have borrowed, carefully abstain from troubling themselves as to the individuality of the last wearer. It will be otherwise, of course, with any who are fortunate enough to possess the facilities at the disposal of La

Reine Margot, the first wife of Henry IV., who did a little tress cultivation on her own account. It is said that this provident Sovereign used to keep little yellow haired pages, and at suitable seasons had their heads shaved to supply material for her wigs. The sources from whence come the hair which one sees worked up into false tresses, chignons, and wigs, can of course be of little interest to the readers whom we now address. It is extremely improbable that the young artist in hair will send or go very far afield for the rough material, (we beg pardon for the use of an expression which must be confined to its technical meaning,) but it may not be uninteresting just to touch upon the heads that once wore the lovely productions we see around us. We will only just touch upon it, as the subject is one leading to paths that had best be left untrodden. Human hair, like most other things, is too frequently offered up by poverty at the shrine of wealth. The young peasant, in many a district, parts with woman's brightest ornament, sometimes to satisfy the necessities of life, and not unfrequently to secure some miserable trinket, which is dear at any price, but inexpressibly dear at such a price as that; yet we hear again and again of such strange barter going on, sometimes amidst scenes of sorrow and of famine, and at others without a pressing necessity, and as a matter not worth a thought. The latter aspect of affairs is however often capable of very easy explanation—cap-wearing. In the Northern parts of France those huge white caps, which astonish a stranger both by their variety and prodigious size, form so important a part of a woman's dress that she may well cease to have any pride in her hair, and she will consequently submit her tresses to the shears without the remotest feeling of regret or shame. The peasant girls of Brittany, for instance, so completely cover their heads with the picturesque caps they wear as to wholly hide the hair, that they are without any inducement to retain it. It is, therefore, not to be surprised at that for years the trade in human hair has been openly carried on in this district. Mr. Francis Trollope, in his "Summer in Brittany," published a few years since, describes a rather amusing scene at a fair in Collenée, where he saw a lot of hair-dealers shearing the peasant girls just like so many sheep. A crowd of fair Brittonese surrounded the operator, and as fast as he sheared he tied the long hair into a wisp, and flung it into a basket beside him Whilst he operated upon one the other girls stood there waiting their turn, each with her cap in her hand.. We can judge how thoroughly callous the fashion of cap-wearing must have made these girls to the loss of their hair, when we mention that the price to each amounts either to a few sous or a bright-coloured cotton handkerchief. False hair has been, however, so much in demand recently that there is every reason to believe and hope that the fair and simple Brittonese have, ere now, become aware of the increased value of the article which they provide for the fashion-market, and that Messieurs, the Shearers, have to come provided with something better than cotton handkerchiefs, however highly coloured. Another well known source of supply is the Convent. The devotee abandons, with all other earthly vanities, the golden or jet black tresses which nature gave to rank among the sweetest of woman's charms. Yet still they are not lost to vanity : they pass into the hands of the hair-dealer, again to appear in that gay world which their owners have renounced for ever, and again to be offered up at the shrine of fashion. It seems hard and ungenerous to bring anything so beautiful as woman's hair down to the rough test of classification, but the hair-dealer tests it as a simple natural production, and, like any other merchant, he can put his finger upon the places in the map where the different shades are produced with as much ease as a dealer in indigo or cotton could point out the districts in which these commodities grow. Look with whatever feelings of loving admiration you may upon beauty, with its most brilliant of honoured adornments, reality still forces itself upon you. Few know that that languishing blonde who passes along captivating all who venture to look upon her, wears, after all, not her own hair, but the golden tresses of some fair young German peasant-girl, or the yellow lock that hung over other shoulders, perhaps as fair as hers, in Holland. Then the dark-eyed, commanding beauty, who comes next, vanquishing even the most obdurate, is also a borrower. The jet black hair is not all a gift from nature to her. It shone, long before she had it, under an Italian or Spanish sun. The extent to which false hair is used in England seems rather alarming, if we are to credit the statement of the " Hair-dresser's Journal," which certainly ought to be an authority on the subject. That organ states that about one in every ten English women wears a greater or less quantity of false hair mixed with her own. Whether this statement be true or false, however, what are we to think of the hair-dresser who betrays the confidence reposed in him by giving such a fact to the world. Nothing would be too bad for so faithless a creature. His hair ought to be combed with one of the most aggravating of his own instruments : it ought to be curled with his own curling-tongs, warmed to a white heat, until there is not a straight hair left upon his head ; and, as a final punishment, he ought to be compelled to listen to his own conversation by the hour together, and be made, not only to purchase and pay for, but also to use large quantities of the most ridiculous specific which he sells. When he has suffered all this we may think of forgiving him. Having disposed of our hair-dresser we willingly return to those whom he has maligned. Assuming that so large a proportion of English ladies indulge in false tresses, what will our readers think when we tell them that the colour most in request is said to be brown. We certainly thought golden reigned supreme, but it would appear not to be so. Among the better classes of English people, however, brown is said to be the prevailing colour ; but then our population is made up of so many races, that we have all sorts of hair. In many parts of the country the descendants of these separate nationalities still retain many of the peculiarities of their races. Among the peasantry of the

South and West the flaxen hair of the Saxon is still
to be seen predominating, whilst in Wales the blue-
black, stated, whether rightly or not we wont stay to
enquire, to be a peculiarity of the Celt, is to be seen
in luxuriant profusion. In the North-Eastern pro-
vinces race is still more strongly marked. There you
find among the common people, who are tied to the
soil, the undoubted red hair of their Danish ancestors.
These various elements appear to have intermingled
in the large towns, and in these, and especially in
London, an average brown tint would seem to be
beyond dispute the prevailing colour. Dr. Beddoes
has stated one ingenious theory, that year by year we
are gradually becoming a darker haired people by
reason of conjugal selection. We give the materials
by which he arrives at the conclusion that our fair
readers may judge for themselves, and determine what
shade of hair offers the best chance in the matri-
monial market. The Doctor examined the heads of
737 women, and he found that of these 22 had red
hair, 95 fair hair, 240 brown, 336 dark brown, and
33 black. We must now follow as many of these
ladies as became the subjects of conjugal selection,
and see how it fared with them. Well, the Doctor
found that of the 367 red, fair, and brown haired

ones, whom he classed as fair, 32 per cent. were single; whilst of the dark ones, comprising the dark brown and black only, 21.5 per cent. are single. This certainly seems to show a preference for dark hair among the marrying men of this country. We do not recommend those of our fair readers who possess golden hair to act upon the result of Dr. Beddoes' enquiry, and dye their tresses a jet black, for after all it must be remembered that however important the colour of hair may be in the selection of a wife, there are other calculations which enter into the mind if not the heart of man, and influence his choice.

Having done our shearing work, and got the hair off the head, we must now follow it to its re-appearance there in an artificial form. It appears to be doubtful whether that glorious red hair, which one sees in the portraits of Queen Elizabeth, was after all her own. The Good Queen Bess is said to have had her head shaved, and to have worn a wig: and as for her cousin, Mary Queen of Scots, she had a most complete collection of wigs, and it is recorded upon the most unimpeachable evidence that she wore one at her execution. Our old and gossiping friend, Samuel Pepys, tells us a good deal about himself and his wig, in that delightful diary of his. In giving an account of his assets and liabilities on the 30th of Oct., 1663, he says, " To my great sorrow I find myself £43 worse than I was the last month, which was then £760, and now it is but £717. But it hath chiefly arisen from my laying out in clothes for myself and wife, viz., for her about £12, and for myself £55, or thereabouts,— having made myself a velvet cloak, two new cloth skirts, black plain both, a new shag gown, trimmed with gold buttons and twist, with a new hat, and silk tops for my legs, and many other things, being resolved henceforward to go like myself; and also two perriwigs, one whereof cost me £3, and the other 40/. I have worn neither yet, but will begin next week, God willing." A few days later he tells us, " I heard the Duke say that he was going to wear a perriwig, and they say the King also will. I never till this day observed that the King is mighty gray." Perriwigs do not seem to have become much of a rage at this time, as we find the entry for the next Sunday in the diary runs thus :—" To Church, when I find that my coming in a perriwig did not prove so strange as I was afraid it would, for I thought that all the Church would presently have cast their eyes upon me. 9th. To the Duke, when we came to his closet he told us that Mr. Pepys was so altered with his new perriwig that he did not know him." Another time he writes, "Went home, and by and by came Chapman, the perriwig-maker, and upon my liking it, without more ado I went up, and then he cut off my hair, which went a little to my heart at present to part with it; but it being over, and my wig on, I paid him £3, and went away, he with my hair to make up another of, and by and by I went abroad, after I had caused all my maids to look upon it, and then concluded it did become me." Following the course of the Diary we find that in 1665 the wearing of perriwigs had a new enemy to contend with in the fear of the plague. On the 3rd Sept.—Lord's Day—Pepys writes:—"Up and put on my coloured silk suit, very fine, and my new perriwig, bought a good while since, but durst not wear, because the plague was in Westminster when I bought it, and it is a wonder what will be the fashion after the plague is done, as to perriwigs, for nobody will dare to buy any haire for fear of the infection, that it had been cut off the heads of people dead of the plague." Although Pepys would wear perriwigs himself, he was less tolerant of the use of artificial hair by his wife. In 1666, March 24th, he writes:—"By and by comes La Belle Pierce to see my wife, and to bring her a pair of perugrees of hair, as the fashion now is for ladies to wear, which are pretty, and are of my wife's own hair, or else I should not endure them." We may doubt whether the locks came originally from the head of the fair lady who wore them. At all events her husband's horror of the artificial seems to have continued, for two or three years afterwards. On the 15th March, 1664, we find—" This day my wife began to wear light-coloured locks, quite white almost, which, though it makes her look very pretty, yet not being natural vexes me, that I will not have her wear them;" and 1666, 4th July, " soon as dined my wife and I went to the Duke's play-house, and there saw Heraclius, an excellent play, to my extraordinary content, and the more from the house being very full, and great company; among others, Mrs. Stewart, very fine, with her locks done up with puffs, as my wife calls them, and several other great ladies had their hair so, though I do not like it, but my wife do mightily, but it is only because she sees it is the fashion."

Whatever the fashion of wearing wigs may have been in 1748, Lord Chesterfield seems, in one instance at least, to have placed nature before art. In one of those letters to his son, once as largely read as they now appear to be forgotten, he tells his dear boy—" I can by no means agree to your cutting off your hair. I am very sure that your head-aches cannot proceed from thence, and as for the pimples upon your head, they are only owing to the heat of the season, and consequently will not last long. But your own hair is at your age such an ornament, and a wig, however well made, such a disguise, that I will on no account whatsoever have you cut off your hair. Nature did not give it you for nothing, still less to cause you the head-ache. Mr. Elliot's hair grew so ill and bushy that he was in the right to cut it off. But you have not the same reason." The wigs worn by gentlemen in the streets of London were frequently of so costly a nature as to offer to a thief all the attractiveness of a gold watch or a diamond pin. When we hear of a wig costing as much as thirty to forty guineas we must not be surprised to hear of many an ingenious theft. A small dog in a butcher's tray poised on the shoulders of a tall man could frequently get through a large amount of business in this way. The wig was adroitly twitched off, and whilst the astonished and dismantled owner looked round for it in vain, the tray-bearer made off, an accomplice impeding the wigless victim under the pretence of assisting him. With wigs at such a price one may account for the story told of the

Duke of Marlborough, after the Battle of Ramillies. Amongst the baggage of the Marshal Vileroy was found his perruque, *à naud espagnol*, and when it was brought to Marlborough the Duke put it on exultingly as his crowning triumph, and in the appropriation of the valuable head-dress was possibly not uninfluenced by motives of economy, which those who regard avarice as his master passion would attribute to him. Kant's wig is said to have been sold immediately after his death for nearly three thousand pounds, and on being put up to auction some years afterwards fetched twelve thousand thalers, or rather more than fifteen hundred pounds.

Whilst wigs were fashionable, the being wigged was as well-defined an approach to manhood as being breeched, and was an event not unfrequently, as it would seem, postponed to as distant a day as possible by careful parents. The wife of Racine thus writes to his son, Jean Baptiste, who on becoming Secretary to the Embassy in Holland was obliged to conform to the prevailing fashion :—" Your father deeply regrets the necessity which you say you are under of wearing a wig. He leaves the decision to the Ambassador. When your father is in better health he will order M. Marguery to make you such a one as you require.

Madame La Comtesse De Gramont is very sorry for you that you should lose the attraction which your hair gave."

There may possibly be a variety of opinions as to how far wigs are ornamental, but of their usefulness we know of but one recorded instance, and even that is of doubtful authenticity. The story goes that an emigrant, on his way to the Back Settlements of North America, was pursued by a savage intent upon scalping him. Just as the grasp of the Indian was upon the head of the unhappy man the wig which he wore came off, and the intended operator was so startled and astounded that he ran off. This may probably be a traveller's tale only, but when we want to establish the utility of wigs it is as well to be content with something less than facts. Of all wigs the most unnecessary, hideous, and absurd contrivance is that worn by the English barrister and judge in the discharge of their forensic and judicial functions. The only thing that this remarkable head-dress has to recommend it is its absolute want of resemblance to any thing else ever seen in nature or art. To look at it one would imagine it to be one of the most ancient head-dresses that ever adorned or disfigured the brows of man, and yet it has nothing in the way of antiquity to boast of: barrister's wigs were unknown in this country before the 17th century, and then they came into use as a French novelty, brought here at the time of the Restoration. Previous to the 17th century the common law judges of England wore, as did their predecessors for many a past generation, not wigs, but velvet caps, coifs and three-cornered caps. Many of the old portraits of our most distinguished English judges, to be seen at the Guildhall of the city of London and the Halls of the Inns of Court, represent the judges as wearing the coif, or coif-cap. The coif, which was made of white lawn or silk, was worn by the common law judges to denote that they belonged to the ancient and learned brotherhood of Sergeants-at-law. " Every of them alwayes," says Fortescue, " while he sitteth in the King's Courts weareth a white quoife of silke, which is the principal and chiefe insignement of habite wherewith Sergeants-at-lawe on their creation are decked. And neither the Justice nor yet the Sergeant shall ever put off the quoife, no not in the King's presence, though he bee in talke with his Majestie's highnesse." William De Bussy, about as notorious a scamp and as dishonest a lawyer as ever lived before his own day or since, found the privilege of wearing his cap at all times and under all circumstances a source of considerable inconvenience at one time during his career. William, like many of the early lawyers, combined law and divinity, and claimed to be at once a Sergeant and a Monk. On being charged in open court with corruption and dishonesty, he endeavoured to remove the coif and display his tonsure, that he might avail himself of his benefit of Clergy. The coif was, however, fixed to its place with strings, and before the disreputable William could succeed in untying these an officer of the Court had him by the throat, and he was dragged off to prison. The coif-cap is still to be seen when the judge passes sentence of death. In old times this flat square dark cap used to hang at the nape of the judge's neck, or the upper part of his shoulder, and whenever he pronounced the awful sentence of the law, consigning a fellow-creature to an ignominious death perhaps for the crime of stealing an article not worth five shillings, he drew up the black cap, covering the whiteness of the coif, and partially concealing his forehead and brows. In the present day the black cap is generally kept concealed by the judge in the writing-desk before him, and on the verdict of guilty being returned by the jury, is taken out and placed on his wig. The judges on other occasions, festive and sometimes ludicrous rather than solemn, wear their three-cornered hats. The Barons of the Court of Exchequer may be seen thus attired on the 9th of November, when the Lord Mayor of London appears before them to ask the Queen's approval of his appointment as Lord Mayor; to claim the privileges of the City; and last, but most important, to ask the Barons to dinner. On these occasions it is to be observed that the three-cornered hats appear to add neither to the comfort nor the dignity of the distinguished persons who wear them. Its tendency to fall off provokes even the judge to anger, and the spectators to merriment.

The coif and cap have dwindled down to very small proportions in the present day. Let any of our fair readers go into the gallery of a Court of Justice, and looking down, like the superior beings they are, upon the judges and sergeants, they may see in the centre of the wig a little black spot placed on a small circular piece of white lawn. These are all that are left of the venerable coif and coif cap. When the French wigs were generally adopted the Sergeants went into the fashion like all the other old coxcombs of the period. They wore the false hair, and their coifs and caps over it. Finding this a cumbersome plan the ancient coverings gradually diminished in size, until they became the little absurdities they now are.

Lawyers having from all time been men of strong conservative tendencies it is not to be wondered at that the fashion of wigs was one, the general adoption of which was not without opposition. Some of the judges, like sensible men, obstinately refused to have anything to do with false hair; whilst others, and we may well imagine their locks were no better than their law, took a foppish delight in the display of the new decoration. The Great Sir Matthew Hale, who lived down to the year 1676, to the very last steadily refused to decorate himself with artificial locks. It was even later before the Chancery Judges took to the wearing of wigs. In the olden days when the Common Law Judges wore coifs and caps, the Lord Chancellor, like the Speaker of the House of Commons, wore a hat. The Lord Keeper Williams, who was the last Clerical Custodian of the Great Seals and the King's Conscience, and who suffered so many buffetings during the Civil War, used to sit in the Court of Chancery in a round conical hat. Mr. Sergeant Bradshaw, who presided at the trial of Charles I., is said to have worn, to protect himself against violence, a thick large-crowned beaver hat, lined with plated steel. Whatever the object of the president may have been the fact that he wore a hat at the trial is undoubted, for do not the lines go thus—

> When England's Monarch once uncovered sat,
> And Bradshaw bullied in a broad-brimmed hat.

As late as the reign of Queen Anne, when three-cornered hats were introduced, a Lord Keeper wore his own hair in Court, instead of a wig, until he received the Sovereign's command to adopt that venerable covering, the full-bottomed wig. Lady Sarah Cooper, writing of her father, says—" The Queen after this was persuaded to trust a Whig Ministry, and in the year 1705, October, she made my father Lord Keeper of the Great Seal, in the 41st year of his age—'tis said the youngest Lord Keeper that had ever been. He looked very young, and wearing his own hair made him appear yet more so, which the Queen observing obliged him to cut it off, telling him the world would say she had given the Seals to a boy." The youthful Lord Keeper did as her Majesty commanded, and on appearing at Court for the first time in a wig he wore an aspect so grave and reverend that the Queen had to look twice at him before she recognised him.

Mr. Jefferson, in his interesting " Book about Lawyers," tells a not very dissimilar story of Lord Hardwicke, who appeared at the Court of George II. in a plain suit of black velvet, with a bag and sword. The King, familiar with the appearance of the Chancellor in a full-bottomed wig and robes, failed to recognise an old friend in the simply-attired elderly gentleman before him. "Sir," said a Lord-in-Waiting, seeing the cold reception given to the Chancellor, "it is Lord Hardwicke." Unfortunately, however, the King was as unfamiliar with the Ex-Chancellor's title as with his appearance, and in a disastrous attempt at affability, and with an affectation of interest, enquired " How long has your Lordship been in town?" At length, however, the Monarch was set right, and apologised frankly, although in bad English and noisy laughter.

Those judges who were opposed to wigs on their own heads were equally opposed to the adoption of the coxcombly contrivances when exhibited on the heads of counsel, and for years prudent junior barristers who desired to stand well with the Court remained out of the fashion and in their own hair. It was difficult to know which Lord Chief Justice Hale hated most, a perriwigged barrister or an armed

attorney. " He was not pleased," says Bishop Bur-
nett, "to see students wear long perriwigs, or attorneys
go with swords, so that such men as would not be
persuaded to part with those vanities, when they went
to him laid them aside, and went as plain as they
could, to avoid the reproof which they knew they must
otherwise expect." Fashion, however, is at all times
irresistable, and notwithstanding the likings or dis-
likings of elderly judges towards the close of the 17th
century barristers almost universally wore wigs in
Court and in society.

Changing again with the fashion, no sooner did
the fine gentlemen of the West End begin to appear
without wigs at ball rooms and places of public
amusement than the gentlemen of the bar ceased to
appear in wigs out of Court. The judges, however,
continued to wear their wigs in ordinary society long
after the Advocates of all grades had ceased to do so.
Lady Eldon induced her husband, shortly after his
elevation to the bench of the Court of Common Pleas,
to ask the King's permission that he might lay aside
his wig on leaving the judgment seat. The petition
was received with no great favour ; the King hesitated,
and the Chief Justice then supported his request by
observing, with the fervour of an old tory as he was,

that the lawyer's wig was a detestable innovation, unknown in the days of James I. and Charles the Martyr, whose judges would have rejected as an insult any proposal that they should assume a head-dress fit only for madmen at masquerades, or mummers at country wakes " What, what !" said the King, and then smiling mischievously, " true, my Lord, Charles the First's judges wore no wigs, but they wore beards— you may do the same if you like. You may please yourself by imitating the old judges as to the head,— you must please me to imitate them as to the chin. You may lay aside your wig, but if you do you must wear your beard." The stately Chancellor would have suffered anything sooner than a beard. It is doubtful, however, whether the King's answer would have been as telling in these days, when many a bushy beard is to be seen under a white wig. Lord Eldon as Chief Justice, and as Chancellor, wore his wig not only on the Bench but in general society. In his own house, however, he gratified his wife by laying it aside, and numerous were the stories told of the attention which the great lawyer bestowed upon that natural hair which afforded his Bessie so much delight. This domestic amiability of the Chancellor led that " first gentleman in Europe," the Prince of Wales, into an observation which we could wish had been left unsaid. On one occasion, when Lord Eldon was firmly supporting the cause of the Princess of Wales, the Prince growled out, " I am not the sort of person to let my hair grow under my wig to please my wife." " Your Royal Highness," responded the dignified Chancellor, " condescends to be personal—I beg leave to withdraw," and retired.

Samuel Rogers, in his table talk, tells a capital story of Lord Ellenborough's wig :—" Lord Ellenborough," says Rogers, " was once about to go on circuit, when Lady Ellenborough said that she should like to accompany him. He replied that he had no objection, provided she did not encumber the carriage with band-boxes, which were his utter abhorrence. During the first day's journey Lord Ellenborough happening to stretch his legs struck his foot against something below the seat; he discovered that it was a band-box. Up went the window, and out went the band-box. The coachman stopped, and the footman thinking that the band-box had tumbled out of the window by some extraordinary chance was going to pick it up, when Lord Ellenborough furiously called out ' Drive on !' the band-box was accordingly left by the ditch side. Having reached the county town

where he was to officiate as a judge, Lord Ellenborough proceeded to array himself for his appearance
in the Court-house. 'Now,' said he, 'where's my
wig?—where *is* my wig?' 'My Lord,' replied his
attendant, 'it was thrown out of the carriage window.'

Notwithstanding the ridicule and abuse from time
to time showered upon it, the barrister's wig seems
destined for many a year yet to come to encumber
the brows and broil the brains of the Advocate. Some
believe in it. Young lawyers, partly because it gives
them an imposing appearance, and mostly because
young ladies are said to admire the forensic costume.
Old birds who have outlived both personal vanity and
all care for the approbation of the fair,—and you may
imagine what their experience of the world must have
been when they arrive at that pass,—know the influence
of horse-hair upon an unwilling witness and impressionable jurymen, and consequently cling to what may
possibly be an advantage. Very eminent men have
railed at the lawyer's wig. " Who," says Lord Campbell, " would have supposed that the grotesque ornament, fit only for an African chief, would be considered
indispensably necessary for the administration of justice in the middle of the 19th century?" Campbell,
when he argued the great privilege case, an occasion

L

on which he spoke for sixteen hours, obtained permission to appear without a wig, but the concession was accompanied by an intimation that it was not to be drawn into a precedent. Since then, now and again, during very sultry summer days when the wigs added to the heat already unbearable of the ill-ventilated country courts, the barristers have been permitted by the judge to lay aside their wigs. On other occasions, however, the old fashion holds its own, and a barrister in Court, however distinguished he may be, if out of wig and gown is "not seen" by the judge.

Before we pass to another branch of our subject we may be permitted to leave the lawyers to themselves, their wigs, and their clients, and dwell for a moment upon the part which human hair has now and then played in human superstition. It is frequently referred to in connection with most strange superstitions. Among the "Depositions from York Castle," published by the Surtee's Society, are to be found the following: "Ann Greene saith that she sometime used a charme for cureing the heart ache, and used it twice in one night unto John Tatterson, of Gargreon, by crossing a garter on his eare, and sayeinge these words—*Boate a God's name*, nine times over. Likewise for paines in the head she requires their water and a locke of their heire, the which she boyles together, and afterwards throwes them in the fire and burnes them, and meddles not with any other diseases." A little further on in the same volume, p. 209, one witch is found saying to another, " If thou canst gett young Thomas Haigh to buy thee three pennyworth of indicoe, and look him in the face when he gives it thee, and *touch his lock*, we shall have power enough to take life." And again there is the deposition—" Mark Humble further saith, that his mother then lying not well, Isabell Thompson tooke some of her haire to medicine her." It is said that the Mahomedan sorcerists in India make use of hair when engaged in casting a devil from an exorcised person : they pluck some hairs off his head, put them in a bottle and burn the bottle. A superstition is said to exist among the Irish peasantry that to burn the hair will occasion all sorts of inconvenience after death, as the risen spirit will have to wander about to find the destroyed hair, and that consequently they carefully bury every particle that may be left after a hair-cutting. The Scotch peasantry on the other hand are said to burn every scrap of hair that may be left about. It is considered unlucky to cast aside or lose the smallest scrap. I have often, says a writer in " Notes and Queries," noticed the careful anxiety of countrywomen in picking up and consuming "each particular hair," and even sweeping up the place where hair had fallen, or been cut, and scrupulously burning the sweepings in the fire. The only explanation they would give of this unusual care was, that if left about the birds would line their nests with the hair, a fatal thing for him or her from whose head it had fallen; and that if a "piget" (magpie) got hold of it for any such purpose, by no means an unlikely circumstance, considering the thievish propensities of the bird, the person's DEATH within a year and a day was sure. The solemn looks and head-shaking accompanying these explanations convinced me that the speakers were in earnest. "This," continues the same writer, "appears to be a fragment of very ancient lore." In "La Motte Fonque's Romance of Sintrum," a lock of the herd's hair cut off with his dagger and thrown by the dwarf afloat over the sea causes the violent storm by which Folko and his wife are detained at the Castle of Bione. In Sir Walter Scott's "Pirate" we have a scene which would point to the existence of a similar superstition in the Shetland Isles. Norma, of the Fitful Head, thus sings to the Spirit of the winds : —

> " *To appease thee* see I *tear*
>   The full grasp of grizzled hair;
>   Oft thy breath hath through it sung,
>   Softening to my magic tongue ;
>   Now 'tis thine to bid it fly
>   Through the wide expanse of sky,
>   'Mid the countless swarms to sail
>   Of wild fowl wheeling on the gale ;
>   Take thy position and rejoice,
>   Spirit thou hast heard my voice.

Norma accompanied these words with the action which they described —*tearing a handful of hair with vehemence from her head, and strewing it upon the wind as she continued her recitation.*"

Almost akin to these superstitions in weirdness, but differing from them in being well authenticated, is the well known phrase of hair standing on end to indicate fear. It is something more than a mere figure of speech. A writer in Notes and Queries says he remembers at the trial of a man for burglary at the York Assizes about 40 years ago something of this sort happening. Burglary at that time was a capital offence, and during the few minutes of suspense whilst the jury were returning into Court to record their verdict intense anxiety was depicted on the prisoner's countenance, his eyes looked wild and prominent, and his hair stood up bristling all over his head, but directly he heard the words " not guilty " his countenance assumed a calm aspect, and his hair lay down quite flat on his head. In the "Memories of Cardinal Pocca, translated by Sir George Head," is an account of hair standing on end from anger rather than fright. The Cardinal had been placed under arrest by the French General (Miollis), and had sent a messenger to Pius VII. to acquaint him with the outrage, "Not more than a few minutes had elapsed since I despatched the report when the door of the room was thrown open with extraordinary violence, and the presence of the Holy Father was abruptly announced to me. I instantly hurried to meet him, and was there eye-witness to a phenomenon that I had frequently heard of but had never seen, namely, the hair of a violently excited man standing erect on his forehead, while the excellent Pontiff, blinded as it were with anger, notwithstanding that I was dressed in the purple soutaine of a Cardinal, did not recognise me, but said with a loud voice, 'Who are you ?—who are you ?'"

We need not report the innumerable instances that are to be found collected of the indistructability of hair. A remarkable one occurs to us as worth mentioning, and which was discovered at Wymondham. The auburn hair of the Countess D'Albini, the wife of the founder of the Abbey there, on her tomb being opened seven hundred years after her burial, was found to be as fine and glossy as if it had just been taken from the head of a living person. A writer in Notes and Queries suggested that all hair becomes red after lying many years in the coffin, and he mentioned that in most cases such hair is described as being either red or auburn. Another correspondent, however, gives a singular piece of evidence which would lead one to doubt whether such a change does generally take place. This writer states that he could testify to the blackness of a long-buried plaited tress, cut from the head of one of the South American Aborigines, and which had been brought to him as a curious relic by his brother. These people when slain by the Spanish invaders were buried where they fell on the sands of the shore above high water mark, and there they may still be seen by those who seek them, the bodies being shrunk and dried, but perfectly preserved. The hair of the Countess D'Albini, which we have already referred to as having lain in the coffin for 700 years, was of a reddish or auburn colour, but of course it is impossible to say what was its colour during life. There are singular stories told of the length to which human hair has grown; in some instances it is said to have reached a length of seven or eight, feet and there would appear to be very good authority for the statement that the hair has been found to continue growing even after death. Walrerus, in the philosophical collections, gives an account of a woman buried at Norimberg, on whose grave being opened forty-three years after her death, there was hair found issuing out plentifully through the clefts of the coffin, and there appeared to be reason for the belief that the coffin had for some time been covered all over with hair. The cover was removed, and the corpse appeared in its perfect shape, but from the crown of the head to the sole of the foot the body was covered over with a thick set hair, long and curled. The sexton, on touching the upper part of the head with his fingers, the whole structure fell at once, leaving nothing in his hand but a handful of hair. There was left neither skull nor bone, yet there was the hair solid and strong enough. In the same collections Mr. Arnold gives an account of a man hanged for theft and gibbeted, and whose body in a little time, and whilst it still hung on the gibbet, became strangely covered with hair.

PART II.

THE ART OF WORKING IN HAIR.

HAVING rambled and gossipped among the ancient and modern wearers and dressers of hair, we come to hair, not as worn but as worked,—to hair disconnected from the head, and associated with the fine arts. When we think of the imperishable nature of human hair we can easily understand the anxiety with which a tress or lock cut from the forehead of a friend who is perhaps long among the dead, or separated from us, not only by miles and miles of ocean, but by new ties and new cares, is preserved. We look upon the few solitary hairs which call back the dear face never more to be seen, scenes never again to be revisited, and incidents long held by the past among its own. It is not surprising, then, that these links which connect us with the past should be treasured, as we see them sometimes turning up neglected and forgotten from some tiny drawer of an escritoire, long thrown aside in the lumber-room; and still more frequently preserved in the trinket, valued not for the goldsmith's art which it displays, but for the few hairs clustering within. Now to the lasting disgrace of those who practice it, there are persons whose greed of gain leaves them no regard for the finer feelings of the living, no respect for the dead. The hair of a departed friend is taken to a tradesman to be worked up into some little device, and what is frequently done is this—the hair may either be too short or not of sufficient quantity for the purpose intended—the tradesman knowing this, does not as he ought to do, suggest another design, but dishonestly matches the hair with other hair perhaps already worked up, and the unhappy dupe lives on in the delusion that he possesses the hair of a friend whose memory he cherishes, whilst he in fact has that of some person whom he has never either seen or heard of. To such an extent is this practice carried on that it is not unusual for artists in hair to have many parts of the usual devices ready made, of various colours and sizes, to answer any demand that may be made upon them. Now we propose to afford a protection against this abuse. There is but one means of doing so, and that is by enabling any one who wishes to preserve hair to do it unassisted. In a word, to become his or her own artist in hair-working. Before the young artist sets out upon the task before her, a word or two upon the form and peculiarities of the human hair may not be out of place here, as it will enable her to appreciate some of the difficulties she may meet with, and suggest to her the means of overcoming them. The human hair is but very rarely cylindrical in form, and appears to be so only in straight hairs. In curled hair the transverse section is elliptical, and it occasionally exhibits a beam-like form, which is to be accounted for by a furrow passing lengthwise down one side of the hair. As far as curling is concerned the flattened form seems the most favourable, the cylindrical the most difficult. We have a good example of this in the crisp woolly hair of the negro, where a very marked flattening is to be observed, the hairs being sometimes as much as two-thirds broader in one direction than the other. In the wool of a sheep, which appears to approach the cylindrical form, the phenomenon of curling is attributed to the transverse inequalities with which the surface of the hair is furrowed. It is difficult to appreciate the strength of the human hair. Possibly in younger and less charming days our fair reader may have had her hair pulled. Children and parents will do such things in days before beauty has acquired the respect due to it. She will then be able to judge of the amount of pulling her fair locks could endure without parting. She may still, however, be unaware of the strength of a single silken hair. It is, to say the least of it, remarkable; hair is also considerably extensile, and most highly elastic. Saussure is said to have found that a human hair, when freed from grease by maceration in an alkaline solution, formed a very delicate hygrometer consequent upon its property of elongating on absorbing moisture.

CLEANSING THE HAIR.

Having now fairly started on our task, the first thing the young artist has to learn is that the lock he or she (we will say she, we like the expression so much) has to fashion must be absolutely free from all impurities. It may seem to be a sort of treason to the adorable or adored one who bore the silken tress to hint that, in its natural state, the hair is not so.

However dark, or fair, or beautiful the hair may be, it has made the acquaintance of oil and dirt in some form or other, and that oil and dirt must be carefully removed before it is to take its place among the fine arts. Once you admit the presence of oil and impurity their removal is an easy matter. All you have to do is, take, say about half a teacup full of hot water, and dissolve in it two small pieces of borax and soda, each about the size of a nut. Into this preparation put the lock of hair, and having left it in the water for about a minute or two, take it out, and carefully spread it on the palette. Having spread the hair carefully out with one hand, hold it firmly to you, and with the other scrape it carefully down from you with the edge of the knife, until you have entirely removed every particle of any sort of impurity. The manner in which the hair is spread out on the palette, held and scraped, can be more readily seen if the reader will refer to diagram No. 1 of the illustrations. Having carefully scraped the hair, then take about half a teacup full of water, dissolve in it about the same quantity of borax as that used on the first occasion, and in this solution rinse the hair, which will then be ready for the next step in the process. Before going further you must take care to have the pallette carefully cleaned, and freed from any grease that may have been left attached to it by the last process. Having seen that this is done the hair should be spread down evenly on the pallette with the edge of the knife, and the uneven or jagged ends cut off. How this is done will be readily seen by reference to No. 2 of the diagrams. The hair having been now cleansed, spread out, and trimmed, is ready for the more delicate manipulations which follow. The next step takes us into the midst of the art or mystery of hair-working, and here we may perhaps be permitted a word or two of gentle monition, it is that each of our little processes should be carefully mastered before the next in succession is attempted. This will lead both to perfection and to peace of mind, both admittedly not undesirable results. If, after this little lecture, the fair and gentle reader will turn to diagram No. 18 (oddly coinciding, we have little doubt, with the number of her own tender summers), she will find a well known and justly-admired design called the Prince of Wales' feather. Now we mean, with the help of your own sweet intelligence, dear young lady, to point out to you the way in which you may produce that and other designs, even prettier than it is. It will be seen that the feather is made up almost entirely of three

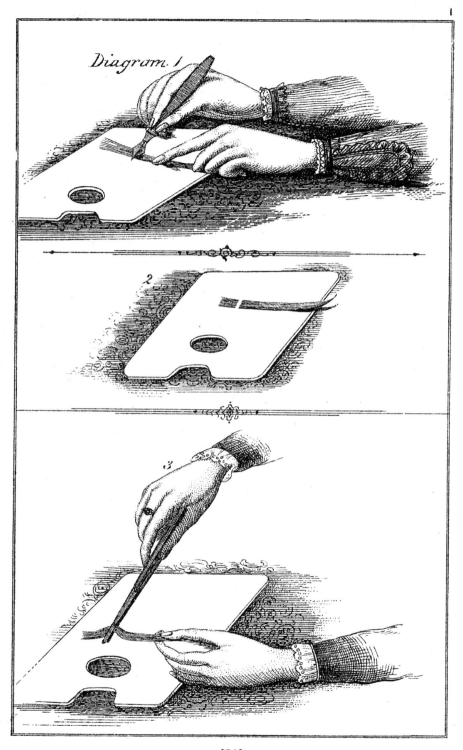

Diagram 1

curls, exactly similar in form. We propose first to show how the curl is produced, and then how the final result, the feather, is attained.

HOW TO MAKE THE CURL.

Take the curling-irons in your right hand, holding the hollow or scooped side downwards. With the left lightly raise the end of the hair, which you will observe by looking at diagram No. 2, ought to hang slightly over the edge of the pallette. That done, put the hair in the irons, and carefully pass them down, until you get to the trimmed end, as in figure 3. Now close the irons as carefully as you can, and turn them round towards yourself three times. You will remember that all this time you must hold the end of the hair carefully in your left hand, keeping it gently stretched round the irons. Then place the irons either in the ·flame of a candle, or over a spirit-lamp, at a point about half way between the handle and the hair, but at such a distance from the hair as to prevent its being injured by the flame, and hold the irons in this position until they become so heated as to cause the

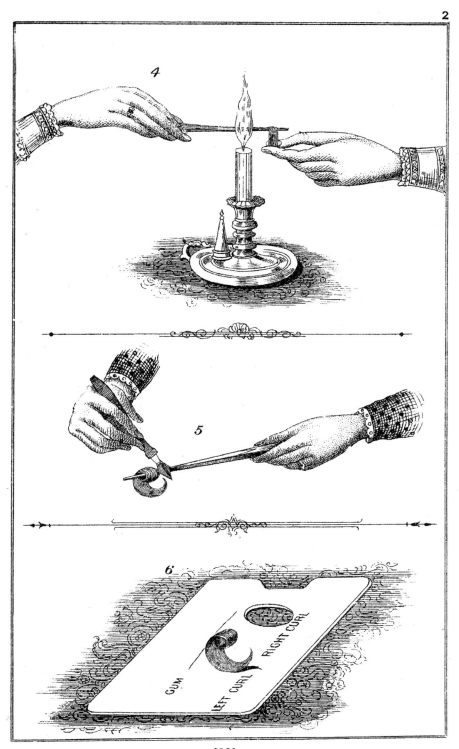

hair to steam. Then remove the irons from the flame to cool. A glance at diagram No. 5 will show how this is done. There is one matter in which you cannot be too careful, and that is to hold the end so firmly and steadily with the left hand that a strong curl may be obtained. Having obtained the curl, the next step is to remove it from the irons. This is a comparatively easy matter, if carefully managed. First pass the irons from the right hand to the left, there is no difficulty in this, for the curl being now set, you need no longer hold the end between your fingers. Then wet your finger and thumb with your lips, and moisten the end of the curl with your finger and thumb, so as to prevent the hairs spreading out, then slightly open the irons, and with the knife gently scrape off the curl on the pallette, as shown in diagram No. 5. The next process is to fix both the ends and twist of the curl by means of a little gum. With a camel-hair pencil lay upon the pallette a fine line of gum ; then lift the curl with the point of the pencil, place the head of the curl on the gum line, leaving the loose end free. Then take a finely-pointed needle, dip it slightly in the gum, pass it lightly through the eye or centre of the curl, keep the curl steadily on the pallette by means of the fore-

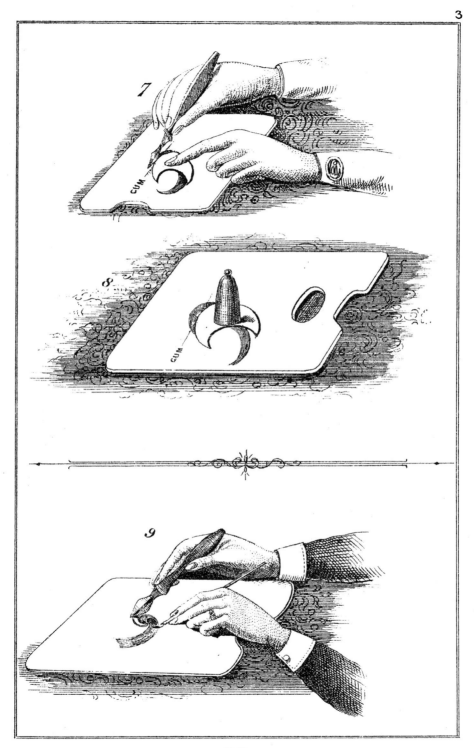

[95]

finger, and whilst you withdraw the needle press it gently, so that the needle may leave a small quantity of the gum inside the curl. Diagram No. 6 will help you to understand the position of the gum-line and curl on the pallette.

Having now made your curl, and gummed it, the next thing is to secure the result of your labours. As soon as the needle has been withdrawn firmly press the curl on to the pallette with the ivory counter, as seen in diagram 7. Then place upon it the sugar-loaf weight, as seen in figure 8, and leave it so for about an hour, at the end of which time the curl will have been sufficiently set.

If you look again at the Prince of Wales' feather on figure 17, you will not fail to observe that one curl turns towards the left, and two to the right, so that in fact you must have right and left curls. This is easily managed, and depends entirely upon which side you insert the gummed needle. For a right curl the needle has to be inserted on the left side, and for a left curl on the right side.

FINISHING OFF THE CURL.

The curl having been made and set in the way we have described, and left under the sugar-loaf

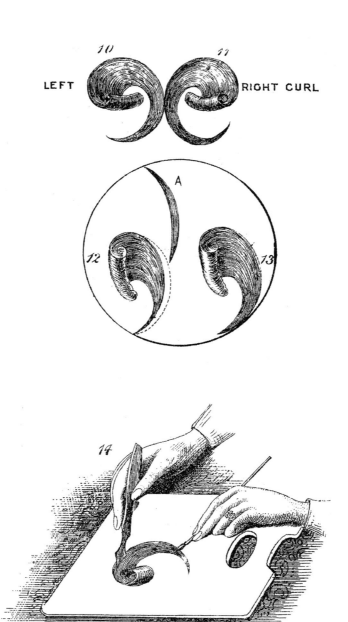

LEFT

RIGHT CURL

weight for an hour, may be finished off. The loose end of the curl is to be freed from any dried particles of gum that may be attached to it, by slightly damping it with the pencil dipped in water, and lightly scraping away the gum with the knife. The loose end having been thus cleansed, should be moistened by the pencil dipped in a weak solution of gum, and the hairs above the curl lightly spread out with the knife, taking a few hairs at a time, and brought round as shown in diagram 9, so as to form figures similar to those seen in diagrams 10 and 11. This done the curl should be slightly moistened with a weak solution of gum, and left to dry in the desired shape.

Now it is just possible that the hair you are anxious to preserve is too short to form a curl of the dimensions shown in the diagrams. In that case we must endeavour to find you a way out of the difficulty, and we think you will see one if you refer to the 12th figure. There you will observe that a deficiency arising from the cause we have mentioned has to be made up. You simply lengthen the curl by adding a tail to it; the dotted lines on figure 12 show you how the tail is attached, and figure 13 represents the completed curl. The curl has now to be removed from the pallette. To do this you warm the pallette by placing it on the hob, or before the fire, for a few minutes, and you will soon find that the curl becomes loose, and may be lifted off with the edge of the knife, ready for either the ivory tablet or opal, in connection with which it must next receive our attention. The next step in the process is to transfer the curls to the tablet, fix them there, and add a few finishing touches for the purpose of giving elegance and lightness to the whole.

Having got a tablet of the size and shape you desire, gum it upon a piece of white writing paper; then take the three curls, one left and two right hand ones, or *visa versa*, according to taste slightly damp the back of each curl with gum, and place them on the tablet, as seen in figures 15, 16, and 17. As far as the hair portion of the design is concerned your labours now have ceased, but as you will observe upon looking at figure 18, there is yet much to be done in the way of finish before the production can meet open criticism. You will observe between the curls two golden ears of barley, and at the bottom of the design a little filagree work and three pearls. We now propose to show you how these are to be prepared and attached, and although the work looks difficult,

and does require some nicety in its manipulation, you
must not be disheartened, for the task, after all, is one
to be learnt with comparative ease. Having provided
yourself with a reel of gold wire thread, wind off about
eighteen inches, and divide this into three or more
pieces of equal length. Now turn to figure 19, and
you will see at the points A and B two small hooks
which are held in the hands of the operator. Affix
the gold thread to the hooks, and make a cord of
them, by twisting the right hand hook, holding the
other tightly in the left hand. Just below figure 19
you can see the result in the form of an enlarged
thread or cord. This cord you may make of any
thickness you please, by simply increasing the number of the threads you use. Having made the cord,
we now come to the next stage of the process. Now
take the tapering needle, twist the cord round it in
the form seen in the 3rd figure of the 19th diagram.
Then pull away the needle, and you have the coil as
seen in the next figure. This coil has now to be
flattened, which is done by simply pressing it down
with a piece of ivory, as seen in figure F. Figure 20
is another form of the coil, and is made, as you will
readily perceive, by pressing the end with a pair of
tweezers into the shape of a figure 8. This is so

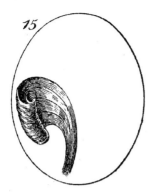

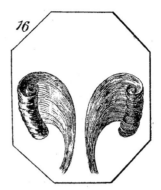

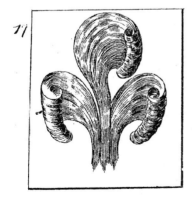

simple and apparent that we need not stop to give any detail of the operation, but go on to the next step.

THE FORMATION OF THE EAR OF BARLEY.

To do this, cut off from the cord, prepared in the manner already pointed out, a piece of the proper length to form the stalk of the barley. Now this must, in the first place, be given the curved form which you will see at figure 22, and the process is quite an easy one. All that is necessary is to hold the piece of cord tightly in the left hand, whilst with the right hand you scrape it firmly between the thumb and the edge of the knife. Then dip the stalk into the gum, and with the camel-hair pencil place it upon the pallette in the position where the ear of barley is to appear. Then fix the stalk into this position by means of the knife, and it is then ready to receive the corns. These are made by cutting the gold cord into little pieces of the requisite length. These having been dipped in the gum are placed along the stalk by means of the camel-hair pencil, side by side, but so as to overlap one another, as seen in the figures 23, 24, and 25 ; and as soon as

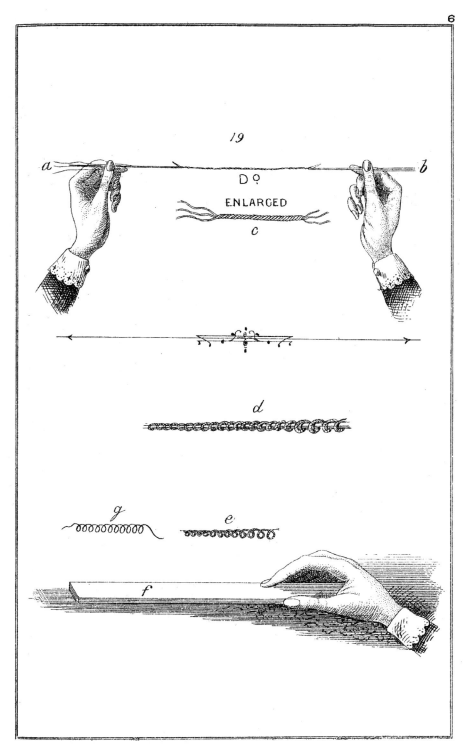

19

D?

ENLARGED

a

b

c

d

g

e

f

you have done that, the barley ears are completed and in their proper position, and we may move on to the next stage of the design. Before we start afresh, however, it is as well that we should remind you that, in all cases, the hair curls must be fixed upon the tablet before you attempt to do anything in the way of golden barley. Having now finished with curls and barley, we may leave them, and go down a little way to the stem of the design, where there has to be formed

THE PEARL BAND

If you will now take the trouble to turn to figures 26, 27, and 28, of the diagrams, you will see the different stages of the bands. First get a piece of white writing paper, cut it into the shape seen on figure 26, and of the proper size. This piece of paper forms the ground work of the band, and should be gummed upon the lower part of the hair, where the three curls join into one stem. You will readily see where this little piece of paper has to be placed, by turning to figure 18. Having affixed the piece of paper, take gold cord, curve it slightly, in the same way you did the barley stalk, and divide it into three pieces, each a little longer than the band. Dip

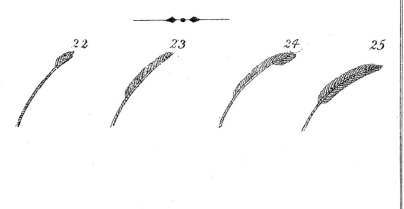

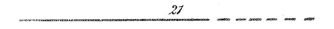

these pieces so prepared into the gum, and place two of them at the top of the band, and one at the bottom, as seen in figure 27. Now you have to add the three pearls, and having done that you will be very near the end of your labours. Take the pearls and split them in halves, by pressing a pin through the hole in the pearl. Dip the pieces of pearl into the gum, and place them one at each end of the band, and one in the centre. By the way it will add considerably to the appearance of the design if you have the half pearl for the centre a little larger than the other two. But one thing more, and we have done. If you look at figure 18 you will observe a little gold filagree work connecting the ends of the two outside curls with the band. Take two pieces of the gold cord twisted into the form of the coils, seen on figures 19 or 20 according to your fancy, dip them in the gum, and place them on the device, in the position indicated on figure 18. A little more and we really have done, and the lesson learnt. Take a little spirits of wine, and by means of the camel-hair pencil slightly damp the design, and with the knife remove any superfluous gum you may see. If you should select an opal tablet, you will do well to place a piece of embossed foil behind it, which will add very greatly to the effect

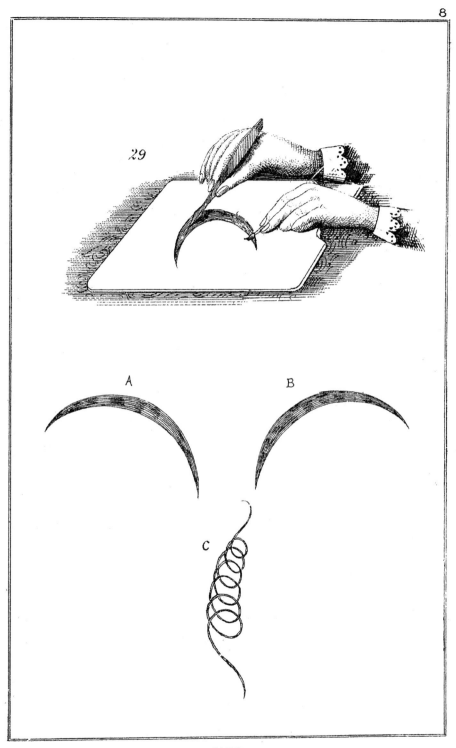

of the whole. It has occurred to us that some of our fair artists might entertain objections both to ears of barley and gold. We will not enquire too deeply into the reason of those prejudices. It is possible that the golden colour of the corn may be too deeply associated in their minds with the filthiness of lucre, or the worldliness of wealth, to desire a place in any thing so purely the creatures of sentiment as hair curls. Whatever it may be we are prepared to respect the feeling and obey the wishes which we guess at, and we consequently are not unprepared to dispense with gold, and fall back upon lovely hair alone. In a word we now purpose to show how the design we have just described may be made with *Sprays of hair*, instead of ears of barley.

If the fair reader will turn to figure 31 she may judge for herself which best suits her taste, gold or hair. If she selects the latter, the means of carrying out the fancy are easy.

TO FORM THE SPRAY.

You should take a small portion of hair, cleansed of course, and moisten it with a thin solution of gum. If you will now turn to the figures on

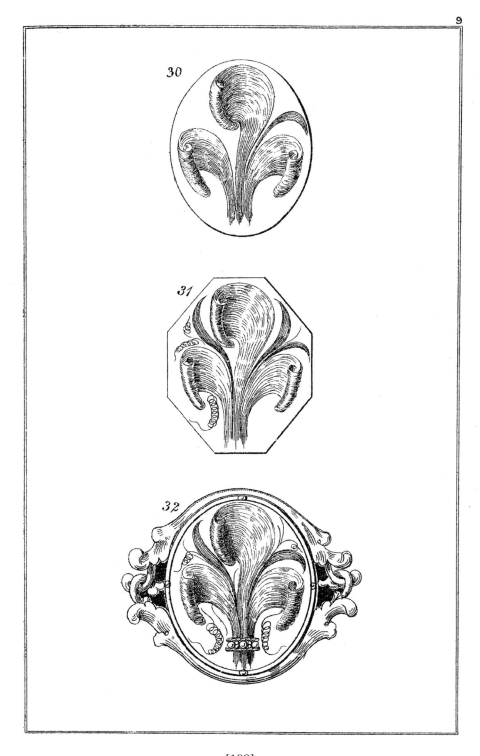

diagram 29 you will see the form of the spray and how it is prepared. Having placed the moistened hair on the tablet by means of the knife, press it into the required shape, and leave it upon the tablet until it is dry. The next thing to be done is to get it off. This is a very simple affair, you have only to warm the tablet, and off it comes. Having taken it off, place it in its proper position on the device just in the same way as you did the ear of barley. At the bottom of diagram 29 you will observe another form of the spray. This is made by taking a small quantity of the cleansed hair, and having moistened it well with stiff gum, working it out to the form seen in the illustration. If care be taken the latter form of spray will be found to add very considerably to the effect of the device. Plates 30, 31, and 32, show the spray as worked in different ways, any one of which the reader may select, according to taste. Having now led our fair young friends through every stage of the Prince of Wales' feather, we will take a final leave of that branch of our subject, and go on to other devices quite as interesting, and, if any thing, less difficult in execution.

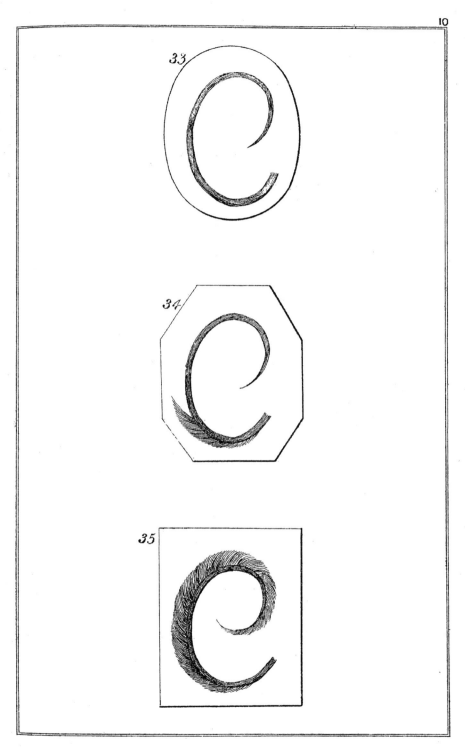

THE FEATHER.

To form the device called the feather, which is to be seen in all its luxuriance in the 38th diagram, we must of course begin with the cleansing, of which we have in preceding pages given a full, and we hope, a lucid account. Having cleansed the hair, the next thing to be done is to select a tablet of the desired shape and size, and by means of a little gum fix it upon a piece of writing paper. Having got so far, and arranged our materials, the first step in the process is the formation of the stem of the feather, To do this take a small quantity of the hair, moisten it well with a solution of gum, place it on the tablet, and then by means of the knife press it into the form seen on figure 33. Here a delay must occur until the hair has had sufficient time to get thoroughly dry and hard. As soon as the stem has become dry, then get some more hair, and cut it into little pieces of about a quarter of an inch in length, or it may be a little more or a little less, according to the size of the device, only, as you will at once see, these little pieces of hair which are to form as it were the fringe of the feather, must be in due proportion to the stalk. These little pieces of hair, which are to form the outer edge of the feather,

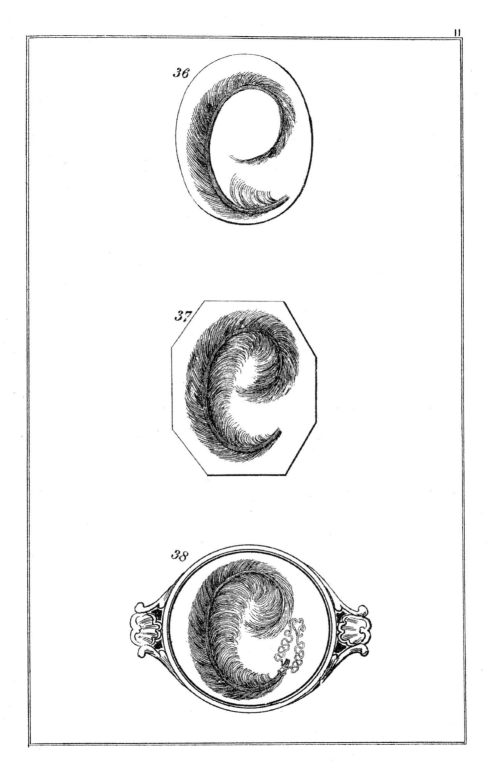

have next to be thoroughly saturated in the solution of gum. As soon as that is done place them along the stem by means of the knife, beginning about half an inch from the bottom, as seen in figure 34, and continue placing them in this way along the stem, using only a few hairs at a time, until the entire outer edge is completed, as seen in figure 35. It is scarcely necessary to point out that the hairs at the top and bottom of the stem are to be shorter, and should gradually increase in length. With the object of imitating the natural form of the feather it is necessary, in addition to the last directions, to observe that in placing the small hairs they should be kept close to the stem at the beginning and end, and gradually spread out and slightly curved towards the middle. Having completed the outer edge of the feather, we must begin again at the inner side, and follow exactly the same course as before. The reader will notice, by referring to the 37th diagram, that the hairs on the inside of the feather, like those on the outside, are short at the beginning and end, and gradually lengthen towards the centre. It will also be noticed that the inner hairs are also somewhat longer than those on the outer side. The feather is now complete, and may be finished off with pearl band and

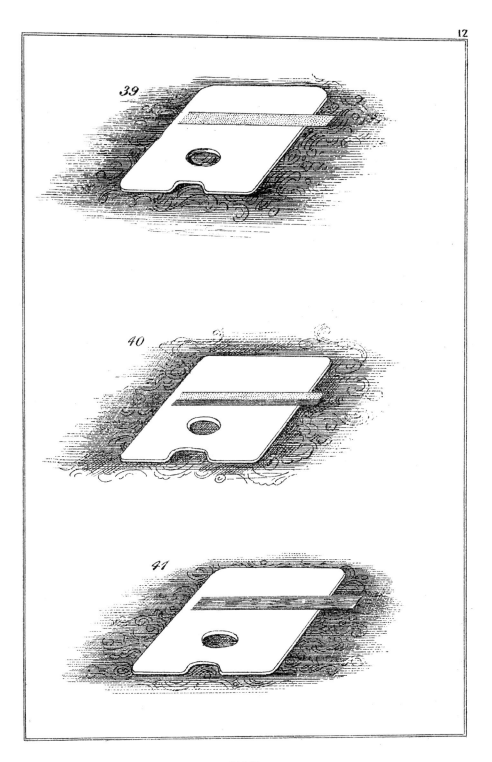

12

[115]

gold tie, as seen in figure 38, and as described in a former page.

PLAITS, FLOWERS, ETC.

We now come to a totally different style in the art of working in hair to that of which we have been treating in the preceding pages. In the interest of the reader we may, however, premise that the designs to which we now propose to call attention are, if anything, simpler and more easy of execution than those which, under our guidance, we hope have already been mastered. With these few words we at once proceed to the formation of plaits, flowers, &c.

We need scarcely remind the reader that as a very first step the hair must be cleansed of all impurities by the means we have already pointed out. That done our fair young artist must provide herself with a small strip of gold-beaters' skin, which she is to place carefully and evenly upon the pallette. Its position will be readily seen if figure 39 of the diagrams be referred to. To place the skin neatly and evenly on the pallette the latter should be slightly damped with clean water. Now having fixed the skin, take some strong gum, and by means of the camel-hair pencil, gum the edge of the skin. Then take a small portion of the cleansed hair, and lay it carefully along the gummed line, in the position seen in figure 40. After which, having carefully arranged the hair in its proper place, press it firmly down upon the skin with the fore-finger of the left hand, and then with the flat side of the knife scrape it down flat and even along the skin. In doing this the great thing to observe is, that the hairs do not cross or overlap each other, but lie side by side smoothly and evenly, as seen in figure 40. Then make another line of gum, place upon it some more hair, and press it into its position in the same way as the first line, and proceed, step by step, until the whole of the strip of skin has been carefully covered, as seen in figure 41. Having completely covered the skin, remove the jagged ends of the hairs with a pair of scissors. Then raise the skin carefully from the pallette by means of the knife, place it between the leaves of a book, put it under some pressure, so as to keep it flat, and leave it until it has thoroughly dried. As soon as you have prepared a sufficient number of slips in the manner above described, and have seen that they are properly dried and ready for use, you may work them up into any one of the designs shown in the later figures of the diagrams.

THE BASKET PLAIT.

This is the simplest design, and certainly the easiest of execution, and to that the fair reader will do well first to direct her attention. In process, and as completed, this neat and effective plait is to be seen in figures 42, 43, 44, and 45 of the diagrams. Take the prepared slips of hair-covered gold-beaters' skin and cut them into smaller slips, of the dimensions you think suitable. Then take a certain number, say seven of the strips, and with some strong gum attach the left ends of the strips to a sheet of writing paper, leaving the other or right ends free, as seen in figure 42. Then leave the strips until the gum has become dry, and they have become firmly attached to the writing paper. As soon as they are ready you proceed to make the plait, which you will at once see, is a very simple operation, and one which requires scarcely any explanation. With a sufficient number of the strips of the same width as those attached to the paper, you proceed to work the plait by taking the first strip and passing it, as seen in figure 42, over strip A

under strip B, over C under D, over E under F, and over G. This done, take another strip and begin again, this time placing the second strip under A over B, under C over D, under E over F, under G, and so on. The third strip will be like No. 1, the fourth like No. 2, and so on, changing alternately until you reach the end, and have made a plait of sufficient size to cover the tablet selected. As soon as the plait is finished carefully raise it up, so as to cover the paper under it with gum. As soon as the gum has been placed upon the paper, carefully put the plait back, press it down upon the gummed surface, so that it shall adhere to the paper, then put the whole between the leaves of a book, put a weight upon the book to keep the plait pressed into its place, and thus leave it until it is dry. As soon as the plait is dry it can be cut into any shape desired. In figure 44 you will perceive it cut into an octagon form, and in 45 you have the same figure set in a brooch. If you will compare figures 43 and 44 it will be observed that the plait can be made with wide or narrow strips, as taste may suggest.

THE FORMATION OF FLOWERS.

We now leave basket work and take to flowers, and if the reader will only turn to the very pretty designs seen in figures 51 and 52, we shall need no other introduction to perhaps one of the prettiest applications of the art of hair-working. The first step of course is the cleansing preparation of the hair, which we will assume to have been completed. That done the artist has to select a tablet of the desired shape, and to fix it with gum upon a piece of writing paper. Now by turning to figure 49, the first stage of the design will be seen. With that before you as a guide take a small portion of hair, and pass it through the solution of gum, which frequent mention will have shown to be indispensable in the working out of any design. Then fix the gummed hair upon the tablet in the curved shape shown in the figure. This forms the stalk of the flower. You have now to add the necessary branches. To do this, take the knife and insert the point at that portion of the stalk whence the first branch is to be taken, and with the point of the knife gently move the branch out from the stalk, and curve it into the proper position, as shown on figure 50. To form the other branches it is only necessary to repeat the last operation, until you have the desired number. Now it is just possible that these branches may weaken the parent tree, and reduce the stalk to an objectionable slenderness. That difficulty is easily got over, like many a one in actual life, by a little patching up. You have only to take a thin strip of prepared hair, draw it through the gum, and place it along the stalk, and the thing is done, and the requisite thickness restored. Having now formed the stalk and branches, we must next direct our attention to the formation of the leaves.

THE FORMATION OF THE LEAVES

It will be remembered that a few pages ago, in talking of basket-work, we described how the hair was to be placed on gold-beaters' skin. Now we will assume that you have some of those strips by you. If not, prepare some in the way already pointed out. Then take the strip and with a pair of scissors cut off a sufficient number of small diamond-shaped pieces. These you will see, on referring to figure 46, are to form the basis of the flower. Now all you have to do is to fix the leaves into their proper positions. To do this take the

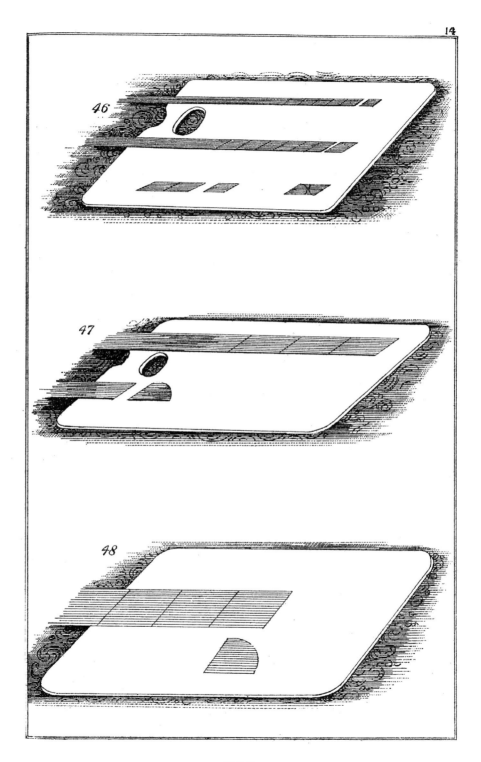

camel hair pencil, dip the top in gum, and with it
touch the diamond-shaped leaves at the extreme point,
and place them on the branches and stalk, and continue to do this until a sufficient number of leaves
have been added to give to the flower as rich a foliage
as you desire it to bear. Having made stem, branches,
and leaves, we have now to add the flower.

THE FLOWER.

This may appear to the young artist a much
more difficult undertaking than it really is. If you
will turn to the *a, b, c, d,* and *e,* on the 15th page
of the diagrams, you will see the flower in its various
stages, and that its formation is, after all, quite as
easy as anything that has already been done. Having
studied carefully these figures, take a small piece of
strong writing paper, and cut it into the circular form
shown at letter *a.* Now you must, before proceeding
any further, depress the centre of this little piece of
paper, so as to form a sort of cup, to give a bed
for the flower. To do this you have only to take the
steel pin, press it firmly into the centre of the paper,
and there is the cup. Then take this little cup and
gum it upon a piece of paper, with the hollow part

uppermost. Now the bed of the flower is ready to receive its leaves. To make these the process is almost similar to that for making the leaves which have already been attached to the branches. Now take one of the strips of hair-covered gold-beaters' skin, lay it on the pallette, and with the knife cut it into pieces like that seen at figure b. Referring to figures 50, 51, and 52 of the diagrams it will be readily seen how the leaves of the flower are formed. On 48 the strips are cut into diamond shapes. On 51 and 52 the diamond shapes are rounded off at one end. This being done with either the knife or scissors, the completed leaf is now represented. Having got a requisite number of leaves, we proceed to make the flower itself. Returning to the little cup, take the camel-hair pencil and paint all the inside of this cup with gum. Then with the same pencil take one of the leaves and place it in the hollow of the cup, as seen on figure b. Then take another and place it beside the first one, so as slightly to overlap it, as in c. Then add a third and a fourth, as in d and e. The flower now only wants its centre to be complete. To make this, take a small slip of cleansed hair, pass it through the gum, and with a pair of scissors cut off a number of fine particles. Take these, place them on the pallette, dip your hair pencil in gum, and with it mould the particles of hair into a sort of little round pea. Place this in the centre of the leaves, and the flower is finished. You may, if your taste should suggest it, place a small white seed in the centre of the petal, and it will be found that this frequently adds much to the finish of the flower. The flower must now be left until it is dry, and as soon as it is, all you have to do is to remove it from the sheet of paper, and fix it with gum on the stalk, in the position indicated in figures 51 and 52. If you will now compare these two figures you will perceive that there is a great deal more finish about one than the other, and that although the basis is the same, there is a bareness and poverty about 51 which is absent in the other figure. This finish is done by painting in between the leaves the buds and additional foliage, seen in 52, and is quite an easy process. Take your camel-hair pencil, and having selected Indian ink for dark hair, or a paint corresponding in colour with any other coloured hair you may have worked, and proceed with the painting.

ANOTHER FORM OF THE FLOWER.

There is another form of the flower to which we now desire to direct attention, viz., that shown on figure 54.

First select your tablet, and having done so, fix it upon a sheet of writing paper. Then take a small portion of the hair cleansed, and drawn through gum in the manner already directed, fix it upon the tablet, and mould it to the shape seen in figure 53, by means pointed out for the formation of the preceding flower. Then cut the stem to the required length, as seen in the figure 53. This done add the diamond-shaped leaves in the manner already pointed out, and the stalk is ready to receive the flower. The flower itself is begun in the same way as the last, the cup of paper depressed in the centre, gummed, and the leaves put on in the mode already pointed out, and seen at figures *g* and *h*, on page 16 of the diagrams. That accomplished, cut four more diamonds a size smaller than the first, round off one end, put some gum on the centre of that portion of the flower already made, and then place the second series of leaves side by side, but slightly overlapping one another, as seen at figure *i*, on the 16th page of the diagrams. In exactly the same way you add four other leaves of a still smaller size, as seen in figure *j*, on the same page. You have now to add the petal, as already directed, and the flower is complete. You now gently lift your flower from the piece of paper, and with some strong gum place it in its proper position on the stalk already prepared to receive it. You can now finish off the whole design, by means of Indian ink or paint, in the manner already pointed out.

Having now led our fair young readers through all the mysteries of curls, feathers, and flowers, we are sure we may venture upon the more ambitious designs seen among the later illustrations.

THE TOMB AND WILLOW TREE.

This very effective design may be studied in its various stages in figures 56, 57, and 58. Here a slight knowledge of drawing becomes useful. Having selected a tablet of the suitable size, and placed it upon a sheet of paper in manner already directed, you begin by drawing upon this tablet the outline of the tomb, as shown on figure 56. Now you can lay aside your drawing pencil for the present. Next take a small portion of the cleansed hair, pass it through the solution of gum, lay it upon the tablet beside the drawing on the tomb, and in the position shown on figure 56. This is to form the stem of the tree. We have next to make the boughs. This is done by means of the knife, with the point of which several single hairs are to be gently moved out into their places, as seen in figure 57. Our next process is to form the willow leaves. To do this take a small portion of the cleansed hair, having first drawn it through the solution of gum, and, with a pair of scissors, cut off a number of small particles of hair. Having secured a sufficient quantity of these tiny pieces of hair, take the camel-hair pencil and distribute them along the boughs, as seen in figures 57 and 58. To form the foliage, take another small portion of the cleansed hair, draw it through the gum, cut it off into short lengths or sprays, and as soon as a sufficient number have been prepared fix them, by means of the camel-hair pencil, at the root of the willow tree, and in the positions marked on the completed design, seen in figure 58. To the left you will observe four small trees. These are formed in the same way as the foliage, with finely-cut hair. The grass may be done with cut hair in the same way, but if done with the pencil, and ink or colour, it will give, if anything, a greater lightness and finish to the work. Having gone so much and so carefully into detail in the preceding pages, we have now barely to touch upon the diagrams left to be described.

THE BASKET OF FLOWERS.

In this may be observed an application of the plaits and flowers already described at so much length. A word or two, however, by way of resumé may be found useful. The tablet is, as usual, to be fixed on a sheet of some of the hair-covered skin, cut it into writing paper. Then the foot of the basket is made by means of the plait already described, and to be seen in figure 42. The foot of the basket disposed of, the body, we need scarcely observe, is formed in exactly the same way, only with plaits of a smaller pattern. The flowers placed within the basket are only our old friends the roses and Forget-me-nots, already described, and to be seen in their various stages in figures 48 and 55. All that remains for us to say concerning them is, that to secure variety it will be well to have the flowers of different sizes. The leaves are of course the same as we have worked with already. It is also telling an old story when we say that the sprays may be made either of hair gummed on, or painted with Indian ink, or paint, care being taken to match the colour of the hair.

<hr>

THE STAR DESIGN.

This, which we commend to our friends of both sexes for its simplicity and beauty, is only another application of the gold-beaters' skin preparation. Take diamond shapes, and set them round, so as to form a circle. Then place over these, and more towards the centre an inner circle of half diamonds. It will be as well to have the star formed of hair of different colours, and we scarcely anticipate any difficulty in this, for we may safely assume that if Bessie should happen to be a golden haired beauty, Edwyn's hair will be of a darkish hue. For the centre piece get a disc of ivory or opal glass, large enough to cover the ends of the inner diamonds. Then fix it in the centre with strong gum, and having so fixed it, write thereon whatever imagination or affection may dictate, or leave it blank. Either course will be perfectly satisfactory. Leaving Edwyn and Bessie united and happy, we pass to another pretty device.

THE WHEAT SHEAF.

To form this, an engraving of which appears as figure 61, you will first have to take some hair, form it into cords, draw it through gum, and place these cords together, letting them come a little thick towards the centre, so as to give a raised appearance. This will form the stalks or straws. The ears of barley may be formed either of twisted gold thread or hair, as already described in figures 21 to 25, and 57. The binding is formed like the stalks of gummed hair, the twist or tie being made of pieces of gummed hair, laid over the binding, two or three other pieces forming the ends of the tie. The foliage or grass may, as previously pointed out, be either painted on the tablet, or made with finely cut hair.

CURLS, FEATHERS, WREATHS, ETC.

The designs represented in figures 62, 63, and 64, it is quite unnecessary for us to point out, are formed in the same manner as the Prince of Wales' feather, seen in diagrams 15 to 18, with curls, flowers, and ears of barley, gold wire, and pearl bands. Diagram 65 is only another form of the Prince of Wales' feather, and needs no further notice, the elegance and extreme tastefulness of the design being abundantly obvious.

Diagram 66 is also a repetition of one of the curls used in making the Prince of Wales' feather, with a spray of hair and feathers attached, whilst it is finished off with pearl tie, ears of barley, and Forget-me-not.

The feathers on figures 66 and 67 are also old friends, but slightly changed in shape, and a little more elegant and finished, perhaps, than when we first made their acquaintance a few pages since, in describing the figures 33 to 38.

No. 67 you will perceive is finished off with flowers, leaves, spray, gold wire and pearl band; while 68 shows a large and small feather finished off with flowers, leaves, and pearl band.

Diagrams 69 and 70 are intended to represent four leaves, and, as will readily be seen, are made of hair prepared on gold-beaters' skin, and cut into the required shape by means of a knife or pair of scissors, and placed along a curved stalk of hair, in the manner already described in speaking of diagram 45.

Diagrams 71, 72, and 73, are designs for wreaths of leaves and flowers, prepared in the way already described, and placed along a line of hair, or a line drawn with a pencil: 73 differs from the others only in having a small feather added.

THE HEART'S EASE.

This elegant device, represented in figure 74, is made like the Forget-me-not, with hair prepared on gold-beaters' skin, cut into the required shape, and gummed on to a piece of paper, prepared as already described, with the stalk and leaves added. We would direct the reader's attention to the form of the leaves, and their number. It will be observed that the flower is formed of five leaves, and that the two leaves behind are intended to be formed of hair darker in shade than that of those in the front. The leaves can be tinted with Indian ink, or any other colour to add to the effect.

THE ASTER.

Figure **75**, representing the Aster, is formed of two rows of leaves of different colours, the lighter ones being placed behind, and tinted. The stem and the leaves in the form of sprays are then added.

THE ROSE.

The design shown in figure 76, needs but little in the way of observation from us, as it will be readily seen that it is formed in the same way as the Forget-me-nots and Roses, already described. The figure at first sight may appear to be somewhat complicated, but if the directions already given are followed it will be found that it can be produced with comparative ease. We would here hint that the leaves had better be made into sections and shapes similar to half ovals, and cut to pattern before being placed on the device.

THE WILD FLOWER.

The centre of the flower, as represented in figure 77, is formed in sections, whilst the two outside flowers are made with hair prepared on gold-beaters' skin, in the manner already described, cut into the required shape and size, and laid flat upon the device.

The cup is formed of finely-cut hair, and the leaves and sprays are added last.

THE TOMB AND WILLOW.

The figures 78, 79, and 80, are only varieties of that described in diagram 58.

THE CURLS.

The device, numbered as figure 81, explains itself. It consists of three curls finished off with a hair tie and one pearl. We have only to add, that if hair of different hues be used it will add very considerably to the effect.

THE GROUP OF FLOWERS.

The very pretty group, shown in figure 82, is formed in the manner already described in working out the various devices previously noticed.

A word or two more upon hair devices and we shall have finished what has been to us a pleasant task. The designs and patterns we have dwelt upon offer to the young artist a large field for the exercise of the gentle art we have been endeavouring to teach. Still, however, we by no mens suggest that attention should be solely confined to the diagrams we have given. It is our hope that the artist may elaborate them, that she may produce combinations of the various patterns, or, led by ambition into untrodden paths, she may, guided by her own good taste, produce designs entirely new.

The selection of the hair with which the designs are to be worked out requires a hint or two. Of course, fineness, and, to a certain extent, length, are, though not absolutely essential, very desirable, and we need scarcely say that if choice were unfettered, the hair of children would be found more easily worked than that of grown persons. We are, however, not insensible to a difficulty here, and we know that in the selection of hair tenderer feelings than mere suitableness will force themselves upon the amateur artist in hair. Well, as there is no resisting these influences, neither would we desire to be thought willing to resist them, we must only meet them, and it after all becomes only a question of design. If the hair be too short for one of the large designs, affection may still have its sway, by falling back upon a smaller pattern. Another word, and we pass on. The hair taken from the nape of the neck will, as a general rule, be found most suitable.

A hint or two about the mounting of the designs may not come amiss. They are usually to be found mounted in the black enamelled gold used for mourning. We suggest that plain or burnished gold should be tried instead, and we will even go further, and recommend that, at all events in their earlier efforts, and with the larger designs, our artists should dispense with any mounting in jewellery at all, but place the work in an ordinary frame, where it will be found to look exceedingly graceful and pretty.

It now only remains for us to bid our fair readers adieu. We hope that in saying what we had to say we have not wearied them. If the lines we have written, or the little art we have attempted to teach, have served either to while away a long winter evening, or to preserve a memento of friendships cemented in youth, and which the rough work of the world has not broken, or to carry the mind back to auburn tresses, or black curly locks, that death has long claimed for his own, we shall not have worked in vain.

A. GOATER, PRINTER, MOUNT STREET WORKS, NOTTINGHAM.

15

56

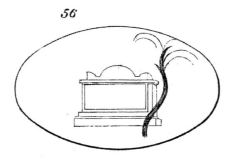

57

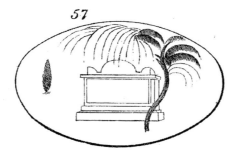

58

IN MEMORY OF

A. B

59

60

ALFRED
AND
JANE
1862

61

62

63

64

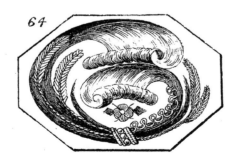

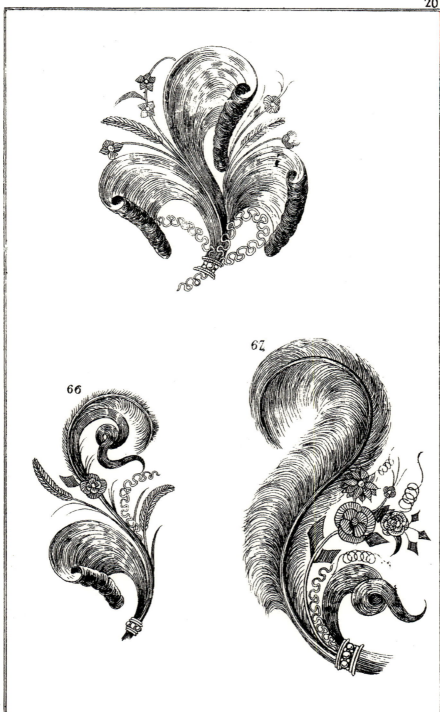

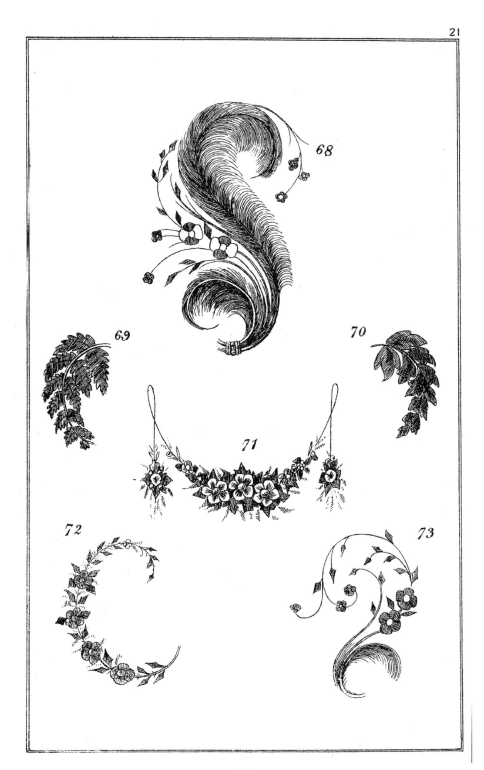

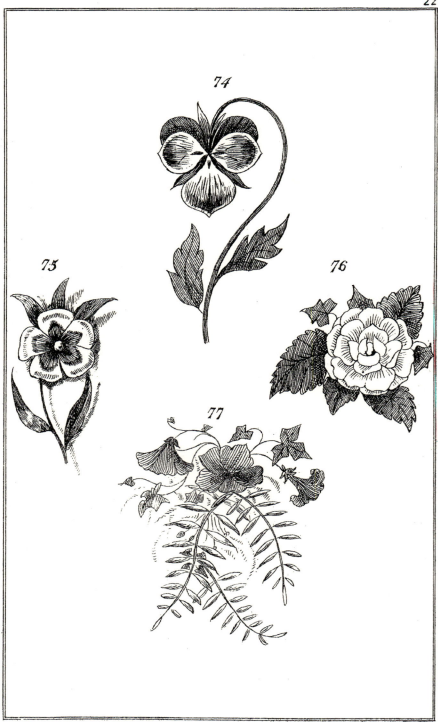

78

79

80

81

82